Welcome Home
QUICK & EASY
COOKBOOK

Welcome Home
QUICK & EASY
COOKBOOK

FUSS-FREE MEALS EVERYONE WILL LOVE!

Hope Comerford

Photos by Bonnie Matthews

Good Books

New York, New York

Good Books books may be purchased in bulk at special discounts for sales promotion, corporate gifts, fund-raising, or educational purposes. Special editions can also be created to specifications. For details, contact the Special Sales Department, Good Books, 307 West 36th Street, 11th Floor, New York, NY 10018 or info@skyhorsepublishing.com.

Good Books is an imprint of Skyhorse Publishing, Inc.®, a Delaware corporation.

Visit our website at www.goodbooks.com.

10 9 8 7 6 5 4 3 2 1

Library of Congress Cataloging-in-Publication Data
Names: Comerford, Hope, author. | Matthews, Bonnie, photographer.
Title: Welcome home quick & easy cookbook: fuss-free meals everyone will
    love! / Hope Comerford; photos by Bonnie Matthews.
Other titles: Welcome home quick and easy cookbook
Description: New York, New York: Good Books, [2024] | Series: Welcome home
    | Includes indexes. | Summary: "127 recipes for stovetop, oven, Instant
    Pot, and slow cooker"—Provided by publisher.
Identifiers: LCCN 2024013434 (print) | LCCN 2024013435 (ebook) | ISBN
    9781680999204 (paperback) | ISBN 9781680999372 (epub)
Subjects: LCSH: Quick and easy cooking. | Smart cookers. | Electric
    cooking, Slow. | LCGFT: Cookbooks.
Classification: LCC TX833.5 .C6464 2024 (print) | LCC TX833.5 (ebook) |
    DDC 641.5/12—dc23/eng/20240327
LC record available at https://lccn.loc.gov/2024013434
LC ebook record available at https://lccn.loc.gov/2024013435

Cover design by Kai Texel
Cover photos by Bonnie Matthews

Print ISBN: 978-1-68099-920-4
Ebook ISBN: 978-1-68099-937-2

Printed in China

Table of Contents

About Welcome Home Family Favorites

Welcome to the *Welcome Home Quick & Easy Cookbook*! Whether you like to cook on the stovetop, in the oven, with your Instant Pot, or in the slow cooker, this book has something for you! If you're looking for something that's quick to assemble, or quick to cook; or if you're looking for an easy-peasy recipe, you'll find 127 of the best to choose from right here in this cookbook. Your time is precious, and knowing you can get a home-cooked meal on the table easily and quickly can take a lot of stress off your shoulders. We are thrilled to help you with that!

As you begin journeying through this book, I always suggest reading it from cover to cover. I can't tell you the good recipes I've passed on in the past by not following this advice. Don't become overwhelmed. Bookmark or dog-ear the pages of the recipes that you think your family would enjoy the most, can be made with ingredients you have around the house, or fit with their dietary needs. Then, when you've looked at everything, go back to those marked pages and narrow it down. Make yourself a grocery list and grab what you don't already have. Voilà! You're ready to get cooking!

Appetizers

Easy Turkey Roll-Ups

Rhoda Atzeff, Lancaster, PA

Makes 12 pieces

Prep. Time: 10 minutes

3 (6-inch) flour tortillas
3 Tbsp. chive and onion cream cheese
12 slices deli shaved turkey breast
¾ cup shredded lettuce

1. Spread tortillas with cream cheese.

2. Top with turkey.

3. Place lettuce on bottom halves of tortillas; roll up.

4. Cut each into 4 pieces and lay flat to serve.

Variations:

Use deli shaved ham and vegetable cream cheese—this is very good!

You can use light cream cheese instead of regular.

Ham & Cheese Crescent Roll-Ups

Sue Pennington, Bridgewater, VA

Makes 8 servings

Prep. Time: 5–10 minutes ⚬ Baking Time: 15–19 minutes

8-oz. can refrigerated
crescent dinner rolls

8 thin slices deli boiled ham

4 thin slices cheddar cheese,
each cut into 4 strips

1. Separate dough into 8 triangles.

2. Place 1 piece of ham on each triangle. Place 2 strips of cheese down center of ham. Fold in edges of ham to match shape of dough triangle.

3. Roll up crescent, ending at tip of triangle. Place with tips down on ungreased baking sheet.

4. Bake at 350°F for 15–19 minutes, or until golden brown. Immediately remove from cookie sheet. Serve warm.

Tangy Cocktail Franks

Linda Sluiter, Schererville, PA

Makes 8–10 servings

Prep. Time: 5 minutes   *Cooking Time: 15 minutes*

12-oz. jar red currant jelly
¼ cup mustard
3 Tbsp. dry sherry
¼ tsp. ground allspice
20-oz. can pineapple chunks, drained
12-oz. pkg. cocktail franks

1. In a saucepan, melt the jelly. Add the mustard, sherry, and allspice.

2. Add the pineapple and cocktail franks to the pan.

3. Cook on medium heat about 10 minutes.

Easy Layered Taco Dip

Lindsey Spencer, Morrow, OH
Jenny R. Unternahrer, Wayland, IA

Makes 8–10 servings

Prep. Time: 15 minutes

8-oz. cream cheese, softened

8-oz. sour cream

8-oz. taco sauce or salsa

Shredded lettuce

Chopped tomato

Chopped green pepper, *optional*

Shredded cheese, cheddar or Mexican Blend

Tortilla chips

1. Blend cream cheese and sour cream until smooth.

2. Spread in bottom of a 9 × 13-inch dish.

3. Layer taco sauce over sour cream mixture, then lettuce, tomato, green pepper (if using), and cheese.

4. Serve with tortilla chips.

Tip:

If you can, add the lettuce, tomato, and cheese at the last minute so the lettuce doesn't get soggy.

Variations:

Instead of salsa, use 1¼-ounce container of taco dip to mix with the cream cheese and sour cream. Add a layer of salsa.

Omit salsa and lettuce. Add 3 tablespoons taco seasoning to the sour cream and cream cheese and add a layer of chopped onion.

Party-Starter Bean Dip

Leona Yoder, Hartville, OH

Fills a 9-inch pie pan (about 15 servings)

Prep. Time: 15 minutes ⚬ *Baking Time: 20 minutes*

16-oz. can refried beans
8-oz. pkg. cream cheese, softened
12-oz. jar salsa, *divided*
Slices of jalapeño peppers, *optional*

1. Preheat oven to 350°F. Spread beans into bottom of a greased 9-inch pie pan or ovenproof dish.

2. Beat cream cheese until creamy in a medium-sized mixing bowl. Add ⅔ cup salsa and beat until smooth.

3. Spread cream cheese mixture over beans. Bake 20 minutes.

4. Let cool 5 minutes.

5. Spread remaining salsa over hot dip and garnish with jalapeño slices, if you wish.

Serving suggestion:

Serve with tortilla, pita, or other sturdy chips.

Nacho Dip

Ranita Reitz, Remington, VA

Makes about 5 cups

Prep. Time: 5 minutes *Cooking Time: 3–10 minutes*

1 lb. Velveeta, or American cheese, cut into small cubes

15-oz. can no-beans chili

1 cup salsa

1. Mix cut-up cheese, chili, and salsa in a microwave-safe bowl.

2. Microwave, covered, on High until heated through, stirring every minute or two.

Serving suggestion:

Serve warm with tortilla chips.

Hot Artichoke and Spinach Dip

Jennifer Archer, Kalona, IA

Makes 2½ cups

Prep. Time: 10 minutes   *Baking Time: 20–25 minutes*

6-oz. jar marinated artichoke hearts, drained

9–11-oz. pkg. frozen creamed spinach, thawed

¼ cup mayonnaise

¼ cup sour cream

½ cup grated Parmesan cheese

1 clove garlic, minced, *optional*

1. Chop artichoke hearts and place in small bowl. Stir in spinach.

2. Fold in mayonnaise and sour cream.

3. Mix in Parmesan cheese, and garlic if you wish.

4. Spoon into a small baking dish. Bake at 350°F for 20–25 minutes, or until bubbly.

Serving suggestion:

Serve warm with tortilla or pita chips.

Fiesta Crab Dip

Amy Bauer, New Ulm, MN

Makes 3 cups
Prep. Time: 15 minutes

8-oz. pkg. cream cheese

1 cup picante sauce

8-oz. pkg. imitation crab

1 cup shredded Mexican cheese

⅓ cup sliced green onions

2 Tbsp. sliced ripe olives

2 Tbsp. diced tomatoes

2 Tbsp. minced fresh cilantro

1. Soften cream cheese and mix with picante sauce.

2. Chop crab and add with cheese and onions. Mix well.

3. Cover and refrigerate.

4. To serve, garnish with olives, tomato, and cilantro.

Serving suggestion:

Serve with crackers.

Guacamole

Joyce Shackelford, Green Bay, WI

Makes 5 cups

Prep. Time: 15 minutes

3 avocados
¼ cup onion, minced
¾ tsp. garlic powder
½ tsp. chili powder
2 Tbsp. lemon juice
1 large ripe tomato, chopped

1. Cut avocados in half and remove seeds. With spoon, scoop out insides and put in medium bowl. Add onion, garlic powder, chili powder, and lemon juice.

2. With a masher, squash avocados until creamy.

3. Fold in tomato, mixing everything together well.

Serving suggestion:
Serve as a dip, sandwich filling, on a salad, or as a garnish.

Breakfasts

Eggs Florentine

Mary Ann Wasick, West Allis, WI

Makes 2 servings

Prep. Time: 10 minutes   *Cooking Time: 5–7 minutes*

l Tbsp. butter

2 cups fresh spinach, torn,
with heavy stems removed

3 large eggs

½ cup milk

Sliced cheese of your choice

1. Melt butter in a nonstick skillet.

2. Maintaining a low heat, add spinach and cover for 2–3 minutes. Stir once or twice.

3. Meanwhile, whisk eggs and milk together in a small bowl.

4. Pour over spinach in skillet.

5. Cook over low heat until eggs are almost set. Then add slices of cheese to cover eggs.

6. Turn off heat, and cover skillet for a minute, or until cheese melts into eggs.

7. Serve, offering salt, pepper, and cubed fresh tomatoes, if you wish.

Elegant Scrambled Eggs

John D. Allen, Rye, CO

Makes 6–8 servings

Prep. Time: 5 minutes ❧ *Cooking Time: 10 minutes*

12 eggs
½ tsp. salt
⅛ tsp. pepper
2 Tbsp. butter
2 Tbsp. whipping cream

1. Combine the first three ingredients in a large bowl. Beat until well mixed.

2. Melt butter in a skillet, making sure the bottom is covered. Add eggs. Have the heat set at medium.

3. Stir constantly until eggs firm up but are not dry. Remove from heat.

4. Stir in the cream. Serve immediately.

California Egg Bake

Leona M. Slabaugh, Apple Creek, OH

Makes 2 servings

Prep. Time: 10–15 minutes   Baking Time: 25–30 minutes

3 eggs
¼ cup sour cream
¼ tsp. salt
1 medium tomato, chopped
1 green onion, sliced
¼ cup shredded cheese

1. In a small bowl, beat eggs, sour cream, and salt.

2. Stir in tomato, onion, and cheese.

3. Pour into greased 2-cup baking dish.

4. Bake at 350°F for 25–30 minutes, or until a knife inserted in center comes out clean.

Southwestern Egg Casserole

Eileen Eash, Lafayette, CO

Makes 12 servings

Prep. Time: 10 minutes   ⚬   Cooking Time: 20 minutes

1 cup water

2½ cups egg substitute

½ cup flour

1 tsp. baking powder

⅛ tsp. salt

⅛ tsp. pepper

2 cups cottage cheese

1½ cups shredded sharp cheddar cheese

¼ cup melted margarine

2 (4-oz.) cans chopped green chilies

1. Place the steaming rack into the bottom of the inner pot and pour in 1 cup of water.

2. Grease a round 7-inch springform pan.

3. Combine the egg substitute, flour, baking powder, salt, and pepper in a mixing bowl. It will be lumpy.

4. Stir in the cheese, margarine, and green chilies then pour into the springform pan.

5. Place the springform pan onto the steaming rack, close the lid, and secure to the locking position. Be sure the vent is turned to sealing. Manually set the cook time for 20 minutes on high pressure.

6. When cook time is up, let the pressure release naturally.

7. Carefully remove the springform pan with the handles of the steaming rack and allow to stand 10 minutes before cutting and serving.

Easy Quiche

Becky Bontrager Horst, Goshen, IN

Makes 6 servings, 1 slice per serving

Prep. Time: 15 minutes ❦ Cooking Time: 25 minutes

1 cup water

Nonstick cooking spray

¼ cup chopped onion

¼ cup chopped mushrooms, *optional*

3 oz. shredded reduced-fat cheddar cheese

2 Tbsp. bacon bits, chopped ham, or browned sausage

4 eggs

¼ tsp. salt

1½ cups nonfat milk

½ cup whole wheat flour

1 Tbsp. trans-fat–free soft margarine

1. Pour the water into the inner pot of the Instant Pot and place the steaming rack inside.

2. Spray a 7-inch round baking pan with nonstick cooking spray.

3. Sprinkle the onion, mushrooms (if using), shredded cheddar, and meat in the cake pan.

4. In a medium bowl, combine the remaining ingredients. Pour them over the meat and vegetables.

5. Place the baking pan onto the steaming rack, close the lid, and secure to the locking position. Be sure the vent is turned to sealing. Set for 25 minutes on Manual at high pressure.

6. Let the pressure release naturally.

7. Carefully remove the cake pan with the handles of the steaming rack and allow to stand for 10 minutes before cutting and serving.

Breakfast Pizza

Jessica Hontz, Coatesville, PA

Makes 8 servings

Prep. Time: 10 minutes ⚶ *Baking/Cooking Time: 25 minutes*

10-oz. refrigerated pizza crust

8 eggs

¼ cup milk or cream

6 slices bacon, cooked crisp and crumbled

2 cups shredded cheddar, or Monterey Jack, cheese

1. Unroll pizza crust onto baking sheet.

2. Bake at 425°F for 10 minutes.

3. Whisk together eggs and milk in a large mixing bowl.

4. Cook in skillet until eggs start to congeal, about 3–4 minutes. Spoon onto crust.

5. Top with bacon and cheese.

6. Bake an additional 10 minutes until eggs are set and crust is golden brown.

Jam Pockets

Jennifer Archer, Kalona, IA

Makes 4 servings

Prep. Time: 15 minutes   Baking Time: 18–20 minutes

8-count tube refrigerated crescent rolls

Flour for work surface

4 Tbsp. cream cheese

4 Tbsp. fruit jam, flavor of your choice

1. Carefully unroll the rolls on lightly floured surface. Divide along dots to form 4 equal rectangles.

2. Gently pinch and smooth dough to eliminate the diagonal dotted lines.

3. Place one tablespoon cream cheese and one tablespoon jam in center of each rectangle. Bring corners to the center and pinch together to seal.

4. Transfer to baking sheet and bake at 400°F for 18–20 minutes.

Variation:

Double the pleasure by placing 1 Tbsp. of cream cheese and 1 Tbsp. of jam on each single triangle (rather than on each rectangle, formed by 2 triangles). Or place 2 Tbsp. of cream cheese and 2 Tbsp. of jam on each rectangle.

Memaw's French Toast

MarJanita Martin, Batesburg, SC

Makes 2–4 servings

Prep. Time: 15 minutes ⚗ *Cooking Time: 14 minutes*

1 cup milk
4 eggs
1 tsp. cinnamon
¼ tsp. nutmeg
½ tsp. honey
1 tsp. vanilla extract
¼ tsp. salt
Dash pepper
4–6 slices of bread

1. Beat all ingredients, except bread, together in a large mixing bowl.

2. Preheat buttered frying pan or griddle.

3. Dip bread in the mixture and put in the pan or on the griddle. Note: Don't let bread soak long in the mixture.

4. Fry on both sides until beautifully browned.

Note:

For crisper French toast, follow instructions. For softer French toast, pour the leftover mixture on top of the pieces of bread once placed in the pan or on the griddle.

Serving suggestions:

Top with flavors such as butter, peanut butter, whipped topping, caramel, or fruit.

Baked Pancakes

Shelia Heil, Lancaster, PA

Makes 5–6 servings

Prep. Time: 5 minutes ⚘ *Cooking Time: 15 minutes*

Your favorite packaged pancake mix for 10–12 pancakes

Water, according to instructions on box

Butter, *optional*

Maple syrup, *optional*

1. In a good-sized mixing bowl, stir water into your favorite packaged pancake mix. Make enough batter for 10–12 pancakes.

2. Pour mixture into greased 9 × 13-inch baking pan. Bake at 400°F for 15 minutes, or until cake is golden brown.

3. Cut into 10 or 12 squares and serve with butter and maple syrup if you wish.

Note:

This is a great recipe when you don't have time to stand at the stove and make piles of pancakes. They taste just as delicious, but allow you time to do whatever else you need to do.

Baked Oatmeal

Lovina Baer, Conrath, WI
Edwina Stoltzfus, Narvon, PA

Makes 8 servings

Prep. Time: 10 minutes ⚬ *Baking Time: 30 minutes*

1 Tbsp. canola oil
½ cup unsweetened applesauce
⅓ cup brown sugar
2 eggs, or 4 egg whites
3 cups uncooked rolled oats
2 tsp. baking powder
1 tsp. cinnamon
1 cup skim milk

1. In a good-sized bowl, stir together oil, applesauce, sugar, and eggs.

2. Add dry ingredients and milk. Mix well.

3. Spray 9 × 13-inch baking pan generously with nonstick cooking spray. Spoon oatmeal mixture into pan.

4. Bake uncovered at 350°F for 30 minutes.

Note:

You can mix this in the evening and refrigerate it overnight. Just pop it in the oven first thing when you get up.

SLOW COOKER

Apple Cinnamon Oatmeal

Hope Comerford, Clinton Township, MI

Makes 2–3 servings

Prep. Time: 5 minutes   Cooking Time: 7 hours   Ideal slow-cooker size: 2-qt.

½ cup steel cut oats
2 cups sweetened vanilla almond milk
1 small apple, peeled, cored and diced
¼ tsp. cinnamon

1. Spray crock with nonstick spray.

2. Place all ingredients into crock and stir lightly.

3. Cover and cook on Low for 7 hours.

Variation:

You can use regular milk. If so, add 1 tsp. vanilla extract and then sweeten each bowl by serving it with a little bit of brown sugar.

Berry Breakfast Parfait

Susan Tjon, Austin, TX

Makes 4 servings

Prep. Time: 15 minutes

2 cups vanilla yogurt
¼ tsp. ground cinnamon
1 cup sliced strawberries
½ cup blueberries
½ cup raspberries
1 cup granola

1. Combine yogurt and cinnamon in small bowl.

2. Combine fruit in medium bowl.

3. For each parfait, layer ¼ cup fruit mixture, then 2 tablespoons granola, followed by ¼ cup yogurt mixture in parfait glass (or whatever container you choose).

4. Repeat layers once more and top with a sprinkling of granola.

MAX FILL
16oz

8oz

Strawberry-Spinach Smoothie

NO-COOK

Hope Comerford, Clinton Township, MI

Makes 1 serving

¾ cup almond milk

½ cup nonfat plain Greek yogurt

2 tsp. honey

½ banana

¼ cup strawberries

1 cup spinach leaves

¼ cup ice

1. Place all ingredients into the blender and blend until smooth.

Variation:

Use any combination of fruit you would like.

Tip:

Have bananas about to go bad and no time to make banana bread? Peel them and slice them in half. Freeze each half individually in baggies, then use them when you're making smoothies.

Main Dishes

Chicken & Turkey

Chicken and Biscuits

Hope Comerford, Clinton Township, MI

Makes 4–6 servings

Prep. Time: 5 minutes & Cooking Time: 6 hours & Ideal slow-cooker size: 3-qt.

2 lb. boneless skinless chicken breasts

10½-oz. can condensed cream of chicken soup

10½-oz. can condensed cream of potato soup

¾ cup milk

½ tsp. salt

⅛ tsp. pepper

2 tsp. garlic powder

2 tsp. onion powder

1 cup frozen mixed vegetables

6 refrigerator biscuits, cooked according to the package directions

1. Place the boneless skinless chicken in the crock.

2. In a bowl, mix the cream of chicken soup, cream of potato soup, milk, salt, pepper, garlic powder, onion powder, and frozen mixed vegetables. Pour this over the chicken.

3. Cover and cook on Low for 6 hours.

4. Shred the chicken between two forks and stir back through the contents of the crock.

5. Ladle the chicken mixture over the biscuits to serve.

OVEN

Parmesan Chicken

Janet Oberholtzer, Ephrata, PA
Cindy Krestynick, Glen Lyon, PA
Susan Roth, Salem, OR
Sherri Mayer, Menomonee Falls, WI
Mary C. Wirth, Lancaster, PA

Makes 6 servings

Prep. Time: 15–20 minutes   ⚬   Baking Time: 20–35 minutes

1 cup grated Parmesan cheese
2 cups fine breadcrumbs
5⅓ Tbsp. (⅔ stick) butter, melted
⅓ cup prepared mustard
6 boneless, skinless chicken breast halves

1. Combine Parmesan cheese, breadcrumbs, and butter in a shallow bowl.

2. Coat chicken breasts with thin layer of mustard and dip into crumb mixture, coating well.

3. As you finish coating each breast, lay it in a greased 9 × 13-inch baking pan.

4. Bake uncovered at 400°F for 20–35 minutes, or until chicken is cooked through.

Serving suggestion:

This would go well paired with Corn Extraordinary, which can be found on page 150.

Variations:

1. Add 1 Tbsp. garlic powder to Step 1, if you wish.

2. Use mayonnaise instead of prepared mustard.

3. Add 1 tsp. Italian seasonings to Step 1, if you wish.

4. You can use frozen breasts, too. Follow the same procedure, but bake 40–50 minutes.

5. For a lower fat version, dip chicken in water, instead of mustard or mayonnaise, before coating with crumbs.

6. Skip the breadcrumbs and butter in Step 1. Instead, mix ½ cup Parmesan cheese with 1 envelope dry Italian salad dressing mix and ½ tsp. garlic powder. Continue with Steps 3 and 4.

Yummy Quick Chicken

Kathleen A. Rogge, Alexandria, IN

Makes 4 servings

Prep. Time: 15 minutes ⚘ *Baking Time: 25 minutes*

½ cup ranch dressing

1 Tbsp. flour

4 boneless, skinless chicken breast halves

¼ cup shredded cheddar cheese

¼ cup grated Parmesan cheese

1. Mix dressing and flour in a shallow bowl.

2. Lightly grease an 8 × 8-inch baking dish.

3. Coat each chicken breast with dressing-flour mixture. As you finish with each piece, place it in baking dish.

4. Mix cheeses together in a small bowl. Sprinkle over chicken.

5. Bake uncovered at 375°F for 25 minutes, or until juices run clear when meat is pricked with a fork.

Serving suggestion:
This would go well paired with Creamed Corn, which can be found on page 152.

Dressed-Up Chicken

Sue Hamilton, Minooka, IL

Makes 4 servings

Prep. Time: 10 minutes   *Baking Time: 10–15 minutes*

1 lb. boneless, skinless, thinly sliced chicken breast cutlets

½ cup ranch salad dressing

5-oz. pkg. potato chips of your choice

1. Lightly grease a 7 × 11-inch baking dish. Preheat the oven to 400°F.

2. Pour ranch dressing into shallow bowl.

3. Crush potato chips, but leave rather coarse. Place in another shallow bowl.

4. Coat chicken on both sides with dressing. Shake off extra dressing.

5. Coat both sides with chips.

6. Place on baking sheet and bake uncovered 10–15 minutes.

Serving suggestion:

This would go well paired with Broccoli with Garlic and Lemon, which can be found on page 154.

Basil Chicken Strips

Melissa Raber, Millersburg, OH

Makes 2 servings

Prep. Time: 10 minutes   Cooking Time: 10 minutes

½ lb. boneless, skinless chicken breasts, cut into ¾-inch-wide strips

2 Tbsp. flour

3 Tbsp. butter

2 Tbsp. red wine vinegar or cider vinegar

½ tsp. dried basil

1. In a large resealable plastic bag, shake chicken strips and flour until coated.

2. In a large skillet over medium high heat, melt butter. Add chicken. Sauté for 5 minutes.

3. Stir in the vinegar and basil. Cook until chicken juices run clear.

Serving suggestion:

This would go well paired with Green Bean and Mushroom Sauté, which can be found on page 163.

Baked Chicken Fingers

Lori Rohrer, Washington Boro, PA

Makes 6 servings

Prep. Time: 10 minutes ⚜ *Baking Time: 20 minutes*

1½ cups fine, dry breadcrumbs

½ cup grated Parmesan cheese

1½ tsp. salt

1 Tbsp. dried thyme

1 Tbsp. dried basil

7 boneless, skinless chicken breast halves, cut into 1½-inch slices

½ cup melted butter

1. Combine breadcrumbs, cheese, salt, and herbs in a shallow bowl. Mix well.

2. Dip chicken pieces in butter, and then into crumb mixture, coating well.

3. Place coated chicken on greased baking sheet in a single layer.

4. Bake at 400°F for 20 minutes.

Serving Suggestion:

This would go well paired with Absolutely Creamy Spinach, which can be found on page 158.

Variations:

1. In Step 1 use 1 Tbsp. garlic powder, 1 Tbsp. chives, 2 tsp. Italian seasoning, 2 tsp. parsley, ½ tsp. onion salt, ½ tsp. pepper, and ¼ tsp. salt (instead of 1½ tsp. salt, 1 Tbsp. thyme, and 1 Tbsp. basil).

2. Use boneless, skinless chicken thighs, and do not cut them into slices. Bake at 350°F for 20 minutes. Turn chicken. Bake an additional 20 minutes.

Chicken with Feta Cheese

Susan Tjon, Austin, TX

Makes 6 servings

Prep. Time: 15 minutes   Baking Time: 35 minutes

6 boneless chicken cutlets

2 Tbsp. lemon juice, *divided*

½ pkg. (about 3 oz.) feta cheese, crumbled

1 red or green bell pepper, chopped

1. Preheat oven to 350°F. Spray 9 × 13-inch baking pan with nonstick cooking spray.

2. Place chicken cutlets in bottom of pan. Sprinkle with 1 tablespoon lemon juice.

3. Crumble feta cheese evenly over the cutlets. Top with remaining tablespoon lemon juice.

4. Bake uncovered for 35 minutes. Sprinkle with chopped pepper before serving.

Serving suggestion:

This would go well paired with Roasted Asparagus, which can be found on page 162.

Jerk-Seasoned Chicken

Louise Bodziony, Sunrise Beach, MO

Makes 4 servings

Prep. Time: 5–10 minutes ❧ Cooking Time: 15–20 minutes

1 lb. boneless, skinless chicken breast halves, cut into ¾ inch-wide strips

2 tsp. Caribbean jerk seasoning

1 pkg. frozen bell pepper and onion stir fry

⅓ cup orange juice

2 tsp. cornstarch

1. Spray large nonstick skillet lightly with cooking spray. Heat over medium heat until hot.

2. Add chicken and jerk seasoning. Cook and stir 5–7 minutes, or until chicken is no longer pink.

3. Add pepper and onion stir fry. Cover and cook 3–5 minutes, or until vegetables are crisp-tender. Stir occasionally.

4. Meanwhile, in a small bowl, combine orange juice and cornstarch. Blend until smooth. Add to mixture in skillet; cook and stir until bubbly and thickened.

Serving suggestion:
This is good served over cooked rice.

Company Chicken

OVEN

Elaine Vigoda, Rochester, NY

Makes 6 servings

Prep. Time: 5–7 minutes ✄ *Baking Time: 25–30 minutes*

1 cup peach jam

¼ cup prepared mustard

1 Tbsp. lemon or lime juice

1 Tbsp. curry powder

6 boneless, skinless chicken breast halves

1. In a small saucepan, mix jam, mustard, juice, and curry. Simmer 5 minutes. (Or mix in a microwave-safe bowl. Cover and microwave on High for 1 minute. Stir. If jam hasn't melted, microwave another 30 seconds. Stir. Repeat until jam melts.)

2. Pat chicken dry and place in 9 × 13-inch baking pan.

3. Pour sauce over chicken.

4. Bake uncovered in a 350°F oven for 10 minutes.

5. Turn each chicken piece to cover with sauce.

6. Cover and continue baking another 10 minutes.

Serving suggestion:
This would go well served alongside Rice-Vermicelli Pilaf, which can be found on page 170.

OVEN

Salsa Chicken

Barbara Smith, Bedford, PA

Makes 4 servings

Prep. Time: 10–15 minutes   *Baking Time: 35–40 minutes*

4 boneless, skinless chicken
breast halves

4 tsp. dry taco seasoning mix

1 cup salsa

1 cup cheddar cheese, shredded

2 Tbsp. sour cream, *optional*

1. Place chicken in a lightly greased 9 × 13-inch baking dish.

2. Sprinkle top and bottom of each breast with taco seasoning.

3. Spoon salsa over chicken.

4. Bake covered at 375°F for 25–30 minutes, or until chicken is tender and juicy. Sprinkle with cheese.

5. Return to oven and continue baking uncovered for 10 minutes, or until cheese is melted and bubbly.

6. Top with sour cream as you serve the chicken, if you wish.

Serving suggestion:
This would go well paired with Hometown Spanish Rice, which can be found on page 167.

Guacamole Chicken

Joy Uhler, Richardson, TX

Makes 4 servings

Prep. Time: 5–10 minutes ❧ Cooking Time: 8–15 minutes

1 lb. chicken tenders, cut into
bite-size pieces

8-oz. pkg. guacamole

1 cup sour cream or plain yogurt

¾ cup salsa

Diced green onions or chives

1. Brown chicken pieces in large skillet sprayed with nonstick cooking spray.

2. Mix in guacamole, sour cream, and salsa. Heat until warm.

3. Garnish with onions or chives.

Serving suggestion:

Serve over rice.

Honey Mustard Chicken GRILL OVEN

Rhoda Nissley, Parkesburg, PA

Makes 4 servings

Prep. Time: 5 minutes ⚬ *Cooking Time: 16–20 minutes*

½ cup Miracle Whip® salad dressing

2 Tbsp. prepared mustard

1 Tbsp. honey

4 boneless, skinless chicken breast halves

1. In a small mixing bowl, stir salad dressing, mustard, and honey together.

2. Place chicken on grill or rack of broiler pan. Brush with half the sauce.

3. Grill or broil 8–10 minutes. Turn and brush with remaining sauce.

4. Continue grilling or broiling 8–10 minutes, or until tender.

Serving suggestion:

This would go well paired with Corn with Bacon, which can be found on page 151.

Chicken and Broccoli Bake

Jan Rankin, Millersville, PA

Makes 6 servings

Prep. Time: 10 minutes   *Baking Time: 30 minutes*

16-oz. bag of chopped broccoli, thawed

3 cups cooked, cut-up chicken breast

2 (10.5-oz.) cans cream of chicken soup

2½ cups milk, *divided*

2 cups buttermilk baking mix

1. In a large mixing bowl, combine broccoli, chicken, soup, and 1 cup of milk. Pour into a lightly greased 9 × 13-inch baking pan.

2. Mix together 1½ cups milk and buttermilk baking mix. Spread over top of mixture in pan.

3. Bake at 450°F for 30 minutes.

Tip:

To cook the chicken, cut 2 large chicken breast halves into 1-inch-square chunks. Place in long microwave-safe dish. Cover with waxed paper. Microwave on High for 4 minutes. Turn over each piece of chicken. Cover and microwave on High for 2 more minutes.

Wild Rice Mushroom Chicken

Karen Waggoner, Joplin, MO

Makes 4 servings

Prep. Time: 10 minutes ⚬ *Cooking Time: 30 minutes*

4 boneless chicken breast halves

2½ Tbsp. butter, *divided*

½ large sweet red bell pepper, or
1 whole small bell pepper, chopped

4½-oz. can sliced mushrooms, drained

6-oz. pkg. long-grain and wild rice mix,
cooked according to directions

Frozen peas, *optional*

1. In a large skillet, sauté chicken in 1½ tablespoons butter for 7–10 minutes on each side, or until meat is no long pink and juices run clear. Remove chicken and keep warm.

2. Melt 1 tablespoon butter in skillet. Sauté red pepper until tender.

3. Stir in mushrooms; heat through.

4. Add rice. Stir in frozen peas if you wish, and steam until hot.

5. Serve mixture over chicken breasts.

Chicken Alfredo Penne

Esther Gingerich, Parnell, IA

Makes 4 servings

Prep. Time: 5–8 minutes *Cooking Time: 15 minutes*

½ lb. uncooked penne pasta

1½ cups frozen sugar snap peas

15-oz. jar Alfredo sauce

2 cups sliced cooked chicken

1. In a large saucepan, cook pasta in boiling water for 6 minutes.

2. Add peas. Return to boil. Cook 4–5 minutes, or until pasta is tender.

3. Drain pasta mixture.

4. Stir in sauce and chicken. Heat over medium heat for a few minutes, just until chicken is heated through. Stir frequently so the penne does not stick and scorch.

 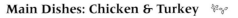

Ground Turkey Cacciatore Spaghetti

Maria Shevlin, Sicklerville, NJ

Makes 6 servings

Prep. Time: 15–20 minutes   Cooking Time: 5 minutes

1 tsp. olive oil

1 medium sweet onion, chopped

3 cloves garlic, minced

1 lb. ground turkey

32-oz. jar spaghetti sauce, or 1 qt. homemade

1 tsp. salt

½ tsp. black pepper

½ tsp. oregano

½ tsp. dried basil

½ tsp. red pepper flakes

1 cup bell pepper strips, mixed colors if desired

1 cup diced mushrooms

13¼-oz. box Dreamfields spaghetti

3 cups chicken bone broth

1. Press the Sauté button on the Instant Pot and add the oil, onion, and garlic to the inner pot.

2. Add in the ground turkey and break it up a little while it browns.

3. Once ground turkey is browned, add in the sauce and seasonings.

4. Add in the bell peppers and mushrooms and give it a stir to mix.

5. Add in the spaghetti—break it in half so it will fit in.

6. Add in the chicken bone broth.

7. Lock lid, make sure the vent is at sealing, and set on Manual at high pressure for 6 minutes.

8. When cook time is up, manually release the pressure.

Serving suggestion:
Top with some fresh grated Parmesan cheese and basil.

INSTANT POT

Turkey Tetrazzini

Hope Comerford, Clinton Township, MI

Makes 6–8 servings

Prep. Time: 10 minutes Cook Time: 3 minutes

2 Tbsp. butter

1 cup chopped onion

1 cup sliced mushrooms

3 cups chicken broth, *divided*

12 oz. wide egg noodles

2 cups chopped leftover turkey

1 cup frozen peas

½ tsp. salt

⅛ tsp. pepper

1 cup half-and-half

1½ cups shredded mozzarella cheese

½ cup grated or shredded Parmesan cheese

1. Set the Instant Pot to the Sauté function. Add the butter.

2. Sauté the onion and mushrooms in the melted butter for 2–3 minutes.

3. Pour in 1 cup of the chicken broth and scrape the bottom of the pot with a wooden spoon or spatula. Press Cancel.

4. Evenly spread the egg noodles around the Instant Pot, not stirring. Just press. Layer the turkey and peas over the top of the noodles and sprinkle with salt and pepper. Pour the remaining 2 cups of broth over the top.

5. Secure the lid and set the vent to sealing. Manually set the cook time for 3 minutes.

6. When the cook time is over, manually release the pressure.

7. When the pin drops, remove the lid and add the half-and-half and cheese, then stir together.

8. Let it sit for a bit to thicken, then serve.

Easy Enchilada Shredded Chicken

SLOW COOKER

Hope Comerford, Clinton Township, MI

Makes 10–14 servings

Prep. Time: 5 minutes   Cooking Time: 5–6 hours   Ideal slow-cooker size: 3- or 5-qt.

5–6 lb. boneless, skinless chicken breast

14½-oz. can petite diced tomatoes

1 medium onion, chopped

8 oz. red enchilada sauce

½ tsp. salt

½ tsp. chili powder

½ tsp. basil

½ tsp. garlic powder

¼ tsp. pepper

1. Place chicken in the crock.

2. Add in the remaining ingredients.

3. Cover and cook on Low for 5–6 hours.

4. Remove chicken and shred it between two forks. Place the shredded chicken back in the crock and stir to mix in the juices.

Serving suggestion:

Serve over salad, brown rice, quinoa, sweet potatoes, nachos, or soft-shell corn tacos. Add a dollop of yogurt and a sprinkle of fresh cilantro.

Soft Chicken Tacos

STOVETOP

Natalia Showalter, Mt. Solon, VA

Makes 5–6 servings

Prep. Time: 15–20 minutes & Cooking Time: 15 minutes

1 lb. boneless, skinless chicken breasts, cubed

15-oz. can black beans, rinsed and drained

1 cup salsa

1 Tbsp. taco seasoning

6 flour tortillas, warmed

1. In nonstick skillet, cook chicken until juices run clear.

2. Add beans, salsa, and seasoning. Heat through.

3. Spoon chicken mixture down center of each tortilla.

4. Garnish with toppings of your choice.

Serving suggestion:
This would go well paired with Corn Extraordinary, which can be found on page 150.

Hawaiian Chicken Tacos

Maria Shevlin, Sicklerville, NJ

Makes 8–10 servings

Prep. Time: 15 minutes   *Cooking Time: 15 minutes*

6 boneless, skinless chicken thighs

20-oz. can crushed pineapple and its juice

½ cup brown sugar

2 (10¾-oz.) cans tomato soup

1 bunch green onions, chopped

Tortillas or hard taco shells, for serving

Optional garnishes:

Sesame seeds

Shredded lettuce

Red onion

1. Add chicken thighs to the bottom of Instant Pot inner pot and add all remaining ingredients on top.

2. Secure the lid and set the vent to sealing. Cook on the Poultry setting for 15 minutes.

3. When cook time is up, let the pressure release naturally for 5 minutes, and then manually release the remaining pressure.

4. When the pin drops, remove the lid. Shred the chicken by using 2 forks directly in the Instant Pot.

5. Add to tortillas or hard taco shells and add any or all the garnishments listed above.

Serving suggestion:

Serve with pineapple fried rice if desired.

Barbecue Chicken Pizza

Hope Comerford, Clinton Township, MI

Makes 6 servings

Prep. Time: 10 minutes ❧ *Cooking Time: 13–15 minutes*

14 oz. premade or homemade pizza dough

½ cup sliced red onion pieces

1 Tbsp. olive oil

1½ cups of your favorite barbecue sauce, *divided*

1½ cups diced rotisserie chicken meat

3 cups mozzarella cheese

⅓ cup chopped fresh cilantro

1. Spread pizza dough on a pizza pan and bake for 5 minutes at whatever temperature the packaging suggests.

2. While the pizza dough is cooking, sauté the red onion pieces in the olive oil until they are translucent. Set aside.

3. When the pizza crust has finished its 5 minutes, remove it.

4. Spread ½ cup of the barbecue sauce over the pizza crust.

5. Toss the rotisserie chicken meat with the remaining barbecue sauce and arrange it on the pizza crust.

6. Arrange the sautéed red onion pieces on the pizza crust.

7. Sprinkle the mozzarella cheese evenly over the toppings on the pizza.

8. Bake the pizza for 8–10 minutes, or until the cheese is melted and crust is golden brown.

9. When you remove the pizza, sprinkle it with the cilantro.

10. Serve and enjoy!

Pork

Carnitas

Hope Comerford, Clinton Township, MI

Makes 12 servings

Prep. Time: 10 minutes ⚭ *Cooking Time: 15 minutes*

2 lb. pork shoulder roast, cut into
1-inch chunks

1½ tsp. kosher salt

½ tsp. pepper

2 tsp. cumin

5 cloves garlic, minced

1 tsp. oregano

3 bay leaves

2 cups chicken stock

1 tsp. lime zest

2 Tbsp. lime juice

12 (6-inch) gluten-free white corn
tortillas, warmed

1. Place all ingredients, except the lime zest, lime juice, and tortillas, into the inner pot of the Instant Pot.

2. Secure the lid and set the vent to sealing. Manually set the cook time for 15 minutes on high pressure.

3. When cook time is up, let the pressure release naturally.

4. Add the lime juice and lime zest to the Inner Pot and stir. You may choose to shred the pork if you wish. Remove the bay leaves.

5. Serve on the white corn tortillas.

Serving suggestion:

This would go great with Hometown
Spanish Rice (page 167) and Southwestern
Cauliflower (page 157).

Zingy Pork Chops

Jean H. Robinson, Cinnaminson, NJ

Makes 4 servings

Prep. Time: 10 minutes ⚬ *Cooking Time: 20–25 minutes*

4 boneless pork loin chops (about 1 pound)

2 Tbsp. olive oil

½ cup apricot preserves, or orange marmalade

Juice and zest of 1 lemon

¼ tsp. salt

½ tsp. white pepper

1 Tbsp. ground ginger, *optional*

1. Brown chops 3 minutes per side in a heavy skillet in about 2 tablespoons olive oil over high heat. Do not crowd the skillet or the chops will steam in their juices rather than brown. It's better to brown them in batches.

2. Remove chops from skillet and keep warm. Reduce heat to low.

3. Add apricot preserves, lemon juice, salt, pepper, and ginger if you wish, to pan drippings, as well as any juice from the pork chop plate.

4. When sauce ingredients are thoroughly blended and hot, return chops to skillet. Spoon sauce over chops. Continue heating until chops are hot but not overcooked.

Serving suggestion:

This would go great when served with Savory Rice on page 168 and Stir-Fried Asparagus on page 160.

Pork Chops with Potatoes and Green Beans

Hope Comerford, Clinton Township, MI

Makes 4 servings

Prep. Time: 8 minutes   *Cooking Time: 13 minutes*

2 Tbsp. olive oil, *divided*

4 boneless pork chops, 1–1½ inches thick

Salt and pepper to taste

1 cup chicken broth

2 lb. baby potatoes, sliced in half

1 lb. fresh green beans, end trimmed

3 cloves garlic, crushed

2 tsp. salt

1 tsp. onion powder

1 tsp. dried rosemary

½ tsp. dried thyme

¼ tsp. pepper

1. Set the Instant Pot to Sauté and let it get hot. Add 1 tablespoon of the oil.

2. Sprinkle each side of the pork chops with salt and pepper. Brown them on each side in the Instant Pot. Remove them when done.

3. Pour in the broth and scrape the bottom of the pot, bringing up any stuck-on bits. Press Cancel.

4. Arrange the pork chops back in the inner pot of the Instant Pot.

5. In a medium bowl, toss the potatoes and green beans with the garlic, salt, onion powder, rosemary, thyme, and pepper. Pour them over the pork chops.

6. Secure the lid and set the vent to sealing. Manually set the cook time for 8 minutes on high pressure.

7. When cook time is up, let the pressure release naturally for 10 minutes, then manually release the remaining pressure.

Raspberry Pork Chops

Louise Bodziony, Sunrise Beach, MO

Makes 4 servings

Prep. Time: 10 minutes ❧ *Cooking Time: 25–30 minutes*

I Tbsp. cooking oil

4 boneless pork loin chops,
½ inch thick

¼ cup raspberry preserves

I tsp. balsamic vinegar

¼ cup raspberries

1. Heat oil in large skillet over medium-high heat until hot. Add pork chops, but don't crowd the skillet. Cook 2–3 minutes or until brown, turning once.

2. Reduce heat to low. Cover and cook 10–15 minutes, or until pork is tender and no longer pink.

3. Meanwhile, in a small saucepan combine preserves and vinegar. Cook over low heat 1–3 minutes, or until thoroughly heated. Stir in raspberries. Serve over pork chops.

Serving suggestion:

This would go well paired along with Sweet Potato Puree, which can be found on page 166.

Tangy Pork Skillet

Sherri Mayer, Menomonee Falls, WI

Makes 4 servings

Prep. Time: 5 minutes   Cooking Time: 15 minutes

4 pork loin chops
¼ cup Italian dressing
¼ cup barbecue sauce
1 tsp. chili powder

1. In a large nonstick skillet, brown pork chops on one side over medium-high heat. If the skillet is full, brown the chops in 2 batches so they brown well.

2. Remove browned chops to platter and keep warm.

3. Add remaining ingredients to pan, stirring to blend. Return all chops to pan, and turn them so the browned side is up.

4. Cover and simmer for 5–8 minutes, or until meat is tender.

Serving suggestion:

This would go well paired alongside Roasted Baby Carrots, which can be found on page 149.

Pork Chop Pizzaiola

Rose-Marie Vieira, ND

Makes 2–4 servings

Prep. Time: 5 minutes ⚶ *Cooking Time: 30 minutes*

3 Tbsp. olive oil

1 Tbsp. butter

2–4 cloves garlic, chopped, or ¼–½ tsp. garlic powder

1 medium onion, chopped, *optional*

1 Tbsp. Italian seasoning

Salt and pepper to taste

2–4 medium-sized pork chops

24 oz. jar of your favorite spaghetti sauce

½ cup sliced pepperoni, *divided*

2¼-oz. can sliced olives

1–2 cups Mexican shredded cheese

½ cup pepperoncini, *optional*

1. Heat up the olive oil in electric skillet set to 350°F, or a large nonstick pan.

2. Drop in the butter to melt.

3. Add garlic and onion; cook until translucent.

4. Sprinkle in seasonings; stir and cook until fragrant.

5. In separate pan, preferably cast-iron, sear the pork chops, cooking until mostly done.

6. Transfer to electric skillet.

7. Add spaghetti sauce, stir all together, heating well.

8. Lay down half of the sliced pepperoni across the top.

9. Sprinkle the sliced olives evenly on top.

10. Spread the cheese evenly on top.

11. Top with pepperoncini, distributing evenly.

12. Cover with lid of electric skillet, or heavy duty foil. You want to create steam to melt the cheese. Heat for about 10 minutes, until cheese melts.

Serving suggestion:
Serve with some hot garlic bread.

Tortellini Carbonara

Monica Yoder, Millersburg, OH

Makes 4 servings

Prep. Time: 2 minutes ❧ *Cooking Time: 25 minutes*

8 bacon strips, cooked and crumbled, or ½ cup prepared cooked and crumbled bacon

1 cup whipping cream

½ cup fresh parsley, chopped

½ cup grated Parmesan, or Romano, cheese

9-oz. pkg. cheese tortellini

1. Combine bacon, cream, parsley, and cheese in a large saucepan. Cook over low heat until hot. Stir frequently to prevent sticking and scorching.

2. Meanwhile, cook tortellini according to package directions. Drain and transfer to a serving dish.

3. Drizzle cheese sauce over tortellini and toss to coat.

INSTANT POT

Sausage, Carrots, Potatoes, and Cabbage

Hope Comerford, Clinton Township, MI

Makes 4 servings

Prep. Time: 5 minutes   *Cooking Time: 10 minutes*

1 Tbsp. olive oil

4 Tbsp. butter

1 large onion, sliced

14-oz. pkg. smoked sausage, sliced

1 cup chicken broth

2 carrots, peeled and chopped

2 lb. red potatoes, chopped

1 small head of cabbage, chopped

1½ tsp. sea salt

1½ tsp. smoked paprika

1 tsp. onion powder

¼ tsp. pepper

1. Set the Instant Pot to the Sauté function and let it get hot. Pour in the oil and butter.

2. Sauté the onion and sausage for about 4 minutes.

3. Pour in the broth and deglaze the bottom of the inner pot, scraping up any stuck-on bits. Press Cancel.

4. Add the remaining ingredients in the order listed.

5. Secure the lid and set the vent to sealing. Manually set the cook time for 6 minutes on high pressure.

6. When cook time is up, manually release the pressure.

Company Ham and Noodles

Diane Eby, Holtwood, PA

Makes 5–6 servings

Prep. Time: 5 minutes   Cooking Time: 10 minutes

¼ cup chopped onion

2 Tbsp. butter

10 oz. fully cooked ham, julienned (about 2 cups)

2 tsp. flour

1 cup sour cream

Hot cooked noodles

Chopped fresh parsley, *optional*

1. In a skillet over medium heat, sauté onion in butter until tender.

2. Add ham. Cook and stir until heated through.

3. Sprinkle with flour and stir for 1 minute.

4. Reduce heat to low. Gradually stir in sour cream.

5. Cook and stir until thickened, about 2–3 minutes.

6. Serve over noodles. Garnish with parsley if you wish.

Serving suggestion:

This would go well paired with Cheesy Cauliflower, which can be found on page 155.

Beef

Herby French Dip Sandwiches

SLOW COOKER

Sara Wichert, Hillsboro, KS

Makes 6–8 servings

Prep. Time: 5 minutes ⚬ *Cooking Time: 5–6 hours* ⚬ *Ideal slow-cooker size: 4-qt.*

3-lb. chuck roast

2 cups water

½ cup gluten-free, low-sodium soy
sauce, or liquid aminos

I tsp. garlic powder

I bay leaf

3–4 whole peppercorns

I tsp. dried rosemary, *optional*

I tsp. dried thyme, *optional*

1. Place roast in the slow cooker.

2. Combine remaining ingredients in a mixing bowl. Pour over meat.

3. Cover and cook on High 5–6 hours, or until meat is tender but not dry.

4. Remove bay leaf and discard. Remove meat from broth and shred with fork. Stir back into sauce.

5. Remove meat from the cooker by large forkfuls.

Serving suggestion:

Serve on French rolls. Serve with Zesty Green Beans, which can be found on page 165.

Philly Cheese Steaks

Michele Ruvola, Vestal, NY

Makes 6 servings

Prep. Time: 15 minutes ⚜ *Cooking Time: 11 minutes*

1 red bell pepper, sliced

1 green bell pepper, sliced

1 onion, sliced

2 cloves garlic, minced

2½ lb. thinly sliced steak

1 tsp. salt

½ tsp. black pepper

0.7-oz. pkg. dry Italian dressing mix

1 cup water

1 beef bouillon cube

6 slices provolone cheese

6 hoagie rolls

1. Put all ingredients in the inner pot of the Instant Pot, except the provolone cheese and rolls.

2. Seal the lid, make sure vent is at sealing. Manually set the cook for 6 minutes on high pressure.

3. When cook time is up, let the pressure release naturally for 10 minutes, then manually release the remaining pressure.

4. Scoop meat and vegetables into rolls.

5. Top with provolone cheese and put on a baking sheet.

6. Broil in oven for 5 minutes.

7. Pour remaining juice in pot into cups for dipping.

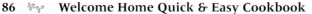

Three-Pepper Steak

Renee Hankins, Narvon, PA

Makes 10 servings

Prep. Time: 15 minutes   ❧   Cooking Time: 15 minutes

3-lb. beef flank steak, cut in ¼–½-inch-thick slices across the grain

3 bell peppers—one red, one orange, and one yellow pepper (or any combination of colors), cut into ¼-inch-thick slices

2 cloves garlic, sliced

1 large onion, sliced

1 tsp. ground cumin

½ tsp. dried oregano

1 bay leaf

¼ cup water

Salt to taste

14½-oz. can diced tomatoes in juice

Jalapeño peppers, sliced, *optional*

1. Place all ingredients into the Instant Pot and stir.

2. Sprinkle with jalapeño pepper slices, if you wish.

3. Secure the lid and make sure vent is set to sealing. Press Manual and set the time for 15 minutes.

4. When cook time is up, let the pressure release naturally for 15 minutes, then perform a quick release of the remaining pressure. Remove bay leaf and discard before serving.

Serving suggestion:

We love this served over noodles, rice, or torn tortillas.

Bistro Steak with Mushrooms

Gaylene Harden, Arlington, IL

Makes 4–6 servings

Prep. Time: 10 minutes   Cooking Time: 20 minutes

1½- to 2-lb. boneless sirloin steak, about 1½-inch thick

¼ tsp. pepper, *optional*

2 Tbsp. oil, *divided*

2 cups sliced fresh mushrooms

10¾-oz. can golden mushroom soup

½ cup dry red wine or beef broth

3 Tbsp. Worcestershire sauce, *optional*

¼ cup water

1. If you wish, rub sides of steak with ¼ tsp. pepper.

2. Heat 1 tablespoon oil over medium-high heat in nonstick skillet. Cook steak about 5 minutes per side for medium-rare, or more or less, depending upon how you like your steak. Transfer steak to platter and keep warm.

3. Stir-fry mushrooms in same skillet in 1 tablespoon oil until browned.

4. Stir in soup, wine or broth, Worcestershire sauce if you wish, and water. Bring to a boil. Simmer for 3 minutes. Stir occasionally.

5. Return steak and juices to skillet. Heat through.

Serving suggestion:

The steak is great served with mashed potatoes—and it offers plenty of gravy.

Slow-Cooker Beef Stroganoff

Becky Fixel, Grosse Pointe Farms, MI

Makes 6–8 servings

Prep. Time: 10 minutes ❧ Cooking Time: 6 hours ❧ Ideal slow-cooker size: 5-qt.

1 cup nonfat plain Greek yogurt

8 oz. cream cheese

¼ cup condensed mushroom soup mix

1 medium onion, minced

4 Tbsp. (½ stick) butter

1 lb. stew beef

⅛ tsp. paprika

8–10 oz. mushrooms, sliced

½ cup milk

1 tsp. salt

1 tsp. pepper

1. Mix yogurt, cream cheese, and mushroom soup mix in medium bowl.

2. Add yogurt mixture as well as all other ingredients to your crock and mix well.

3. Cover and cook on Low for 6 hours. You may stir occasionally.

Serving suggestion:

Serve over egg noodles, or alongside mashed potatoes with Green Bean and Mushroom Sauté, which can be found on page 163.

Easy Pleasing Meat Loaf

Barb Shirk, Hawkins, WI

Makes 8 servings

Prep. Time: 10 minutes ❧ *Baking Time: 1 hour*

2 eggs, beaten
2 lb. lean ground beef
6-oz. pkg. stuffing mix for chicken
1 cup water
½ cup barbecue sauce, *divided*

1. In a small bowl, beat eggs slightly with a fork.

2. Place beef, stuffing mix, water, beaten eggs, and ¼ cup barbecue sauce in a large bowl. Mix with a wooden spoon or your hands just until blended.

3. Shape meat into an oval loaf. Place in a 9 × 13-inch baking pan.

4. Top meat with remaining ¼ cup barbecue sauce.

5. Bake 1 hour, or until cooked through.

Serving suggestion:
This would be great paired with Roasted Asparagus on page 162 and Sweet Potato Puree on page 166.

Barbecue Beef Cups

Jennifer Archer, Kalona, IA

Makes 4–5 servings

Prep. Time: 15 minutes ❧ Baking Time: 10–12 minutes

1 lb. ground beef or pork
½ cup barbecue sauce
1 tube of 8–10 refrigerator biscuits
¾ cup shredded cheddar cheese

1. Brown meat and drain.

2. Add barbecue sauce and mix well.

3. Place an unbaked biscuit into the cup of a muffin tin, pressing to cover bottom and sides of cup. Spoon meat mixture into the biscuit cups.

4. Sprinkle with cheese.

5. Bake at 400°F for 10–12 minutes.

Serving suggestion:

This would be great served alongside Southwestern Cauliflower on page 157.

INSTANT POT

Spaghetti and Meatballs

Hope Comerford, Clinton Township, MI

Makes 6 servings

Prep. Time: 5 minutes ⚬ *Cooking Time: 10 minutes*

1 lb. frozen meatballs

8 oz. uncooked spaghetti pasta

14½-oz. can diced tomatoes with basil, garlic, and oregano

3 cups water

24 oz. of your favorite pasta sauce

1. Pour the meatballs into the inner pot and spread around evenly.

2. Break the pasta in half and place over meatballs in a random pattern to help keep them from clumping all together.

3. Pour the diced tomatoes over the top of the pasta.

4. Pour in the water.

5. Pour in the pasta sauce evenly over the top. Make sure the pasta is completely submerged and push any under that may not yet be covered. DO NOT STIR.

6. Secure the lid and set the vent to sealing.

7. Manually set the cook time for 10 minutes on high pressure.

8. When cook time is up, manually release the pressure.

9. When the pin drops, remove the lid and stir.

Serving suggestion:
Serve with grated Parmesan cheese.

Can't-Get-Easier Casserole

Patricia Andreas, Wausau, WI

Makes 4 servings

Prep. Time: 5–7 minutes ❧ *Cooking Time: 10–15 minutes*

1 lb. ground beef

1 small onion, diced

1 can tomato soup

1 can corn, or your favorite canned vegetable, drained

8-oz. pkg. your favorite dry pasta

Shredded cheese, *optional*

1. In a large skillet, brown ground beef and diced onion. Drain off drippings if necessary.

2. Add tomato soup and drained corn to browned meat.

3. Meanwhile, cook pasta in a saucepan according to package directions until al dente (firm but not hard). Drain.

4. Add pasta to meat mixture. Stir gently and add cheese if you wish.

Tip:

Add ½ cup salsa and 2 tsp. onion flakes to Step 2, for more flavor.

20-Minute Cheeseburger Rice

Peggy Clark, Burrton, KS

Makes 4 servings

Prep. Time: 5 minutes ⚬ *Cooking Time: 15 minutes*

1 lb. ground beef

1¾ cups water

⅔ cup ketchup

1 Tbsp. prepared mustard

2 cups uncooked instant rice

1 cup shredded cheddar cheese

1. Brown beef in a large nonstick skillet. Drain off drippings.

2. Add water, ketchup, and mustard. Stir well. Bring to a boil.

3. Stir in rice. Sprinkle with cheese. Cover.

4. Cook on low heat for 5 minutes.

Serving suggestion:

This would be great paired with Cheesy Cauliflower, which can be found on page 155.

STOVETOP

Un-Stuffed Peppers

Pat Bechtel, Dillsburg, PA
Sharon Miller, Holmesville, OH

Makes 6 servings

Prep. Time: 10–12 minutes ❧ *Cooking Time: 25 minutes*

1 lb. ground beef
10-oz. jar spaghetti sauce
2 Tbsp. barbecue sauce, *optional*
2 large green peppers, coarsely chopped (3–4 cups)
1¼ cups water
1 cup instant rice

1. In a 12-inch nonstick skillet, brown ground beef. Drain off drippings.

2. Stir in all remaining ingredients. Bring to a boil over high heat.

3. Reduce heat to medium-low heat and cook, covered, for 20 minutes, or until liquid is absorbed and rice is tender.

Variation:

Instead of spaghetti sauce and water, substitute 4 cups tomato juice or V-8 juice.

Quick and Easy Tacos

Audrey Romonosky, Austin, TX

Makes 4–6 servings

Prep. Time: 5 minutes ⚹ Cooking Time: 20 minutes

1 lb. ground beef

1 cup frozen corn

½–1 cup salsa or picante sauce, according to your taste preference

10–12 tortillas

Guacamole, *optional*

1½ cups grated cheddar cheese, *optional*

1. Brown ground beef in a skillet. Drain off drippings.

2. Add frozen corn and salsa. Cover and simmer 5–10 minutes.

3. Spoon into tortillas and garnish with guacamole and with cheese, if you wish.

Serving suggestion:

This would go well paired with Hometown Spanish Rice, which can be found on page 167.

Tortilla Chip Quick Dish

Cheryl Martin, Turin, NY

Makes 6 servings

*Prep. Time: 10 minutes * *Baking Time: 8–10 minutes*

I lb. ground beef or turkey, browned
I pkg. taco seasoning
16-oz. can refried beans
¾ cup water
7 oz. tortilla chips
I cup grated cheese

1. Brown meat in a skillet. Drain off drippings.

2. Add taco seasoning, refried beans, and water to browned meat. Mix.

3. Place chips in a lightly greased 9 × 13-inch baking dish. Spoon bean mixture over chips.

4. Sprinkle cheese over all.

5. Bake at 350°F for 8–10 minutes, or until cheese is bubbly.

Biscuit Tostadas

Angie Clemens, Dayton, VA

Makes 16 servings

Prep. Time: 5 minutes ♣ *Cooking Time: 15–17 minutes*

1 lb. ground beef

1 ½ cups salsa

7.3-oz. tube refrigerated large biscuits

2 cups shredded lettuce

2 cups shredded cheese (your choice of cheddar, Colby, or Monterey Jack)

1. Brown hamburger in a skillet. Drain off drippings.

2. Stir in salsa. Heat through.

3. Meanwhile, split each biscuit in half and flatten into 4-inch rounds.

4. Place biscuit halves on ungreased cookie sheet. Bake at 350°F for 10–12 minutes, or until golden brown.

5. Top with meat-salsa mixture, lettuce, and cheese. Serve immediately.

Bubble Pizza

Jeannine Janzen, Elbing, KS

Makes 4–6 servings

Prep. Time: 20 minutes ⚘ Cooking Time: 30 minutes

½ lb. hamburger

3 cans refrigerated biscuits

1½ cups pizza sauce

½ cup sliced pepperoni

1½ cups shredded mozzarella cheese

Optional toppings:

Green pepper

Mushrooms

Ham

Bacon, etc.

1. Brown hamburger in a skillet. Drain off drippings.

2. Meanwhile, cut each biscuit into fourths. Separate pieces and toss into a greased 9 × 13-inch pan, covering the bottom.

3. Spoon pizza sauce over biscuits.

4. Spoon hamburger and pepperoni (and any optional toppings you choose) over sauce.

5. Top with cheese.

6. Bake at 350°F for 30 minutes, or until cheese is melted and slightly brown.

Meatless

Pasta with Fresh Tomatoes and Basil

STOVETOP

Naomi Cunningham, Arlington, KS

Makes 2 servings

Prep. Time: 5 minutes   Standing Time: 2–3 hours   Cooking Time: 15 minutes

2 large fresh tomatoes, chopped

2 Tbsp. snipped fresh basil,
or 2 tsp. dried basil

1 clove garlic, minced

¼ tsp. pepper

4 oz. dry bow tie or other pasta,
cooked and drained

Additional fresh basil, *optional*

1. Combine the tomatoes, basil, garlic, and pepper in a mixing bowl.

2. Set aside at room temperature for several hours.

3. Serve over hot cooked pasta.

4. Garnish with additional basil if you wish.

Meatless Ziti

Hope Comerford, Clinton Township, MI

Makes 8 servings

Prep. Time: 10 minutes ⚬ *Cooking Time: 3 minutes*

1 Tbsp. olive oil

1 small onion, chopped

3 cups water, *divided*

15-oz. can crushed tomatoes

8-oz. can tomato sauce

1½ tsp. Italian seasoning

1 tsp. garlic powder

1 tsp. onion powder

1 tsp. sea salt

¼ tsp. pepper

12 oz. ziti

1–2 cups shredded mozzarella cheese

Serving suggestion:
This would go well paired with Broccoli with Garlic and Lemon, which can be found on page 154.

1. Set the Instant Pot to the Sauté function and heat the olive oil.

2. When the oil is hot, sauté the onion for 3–5 minutes, or until translucent.

3. Pour in 1 cup of the water and scrape any bits from the bottom of the inner pot with a wooden spoon or spatula.

4. In a bowl, mix the crushed tomatoes, tomato sauce, Italian seasoning, garlic powder, onion powder, sea salt, and pepper. Pour 1 cup of this in the inner pot and stir.

5. Pour in the ziti. Press it down so it's in there evenly, but do not stir.

6. Pour the remaining pasta sauce and water evenly over the top. Again, do not stir.

7. Secure the lid and set the vent to sealing. Manually set the cook time for 3 minutes.

8. When the cook time is over, let the pressure release naturally for 10 minutes, then manually release the remaining pressure.

9. When the pin drops, remove the lid and stir in the shredded mozzarella. This will thicken as it sits a bit.

Macaroni and Cheese

Hope Comerford, Clinton Township, MI

Makes 8 servings

Prep. Time: 5 minutes ⚬ Cooking Time: 4 minutes

I lb. uncooked elbow macaroni

2 cups water

2 cups chicken or vegetable broth

4 Tbsp. butter

I tsp. salt

½ tsp. pepper

I tsp. hot sauce

I tsp. mustard powder

½–I cup heavy cream or milk

I cup shredded Gouda

I cup shredded sharp cheddar cheese

I cup shredded Monterey Jack cheese

1. Place the macaroni, water, broth, butter, salt, pepper, hot sauce, and mustard powder into the inner pot of the Instant Pot.

2. Secure the lid and set the vent to sealing. Manually set the cook time for 4 minutes.

3. When the cook time is over, manually release the pressure.

4. When the pin drops, remove the lid and stir in the cream, starting with ½ cup. Begin stirring in the shredded cheese, 1 cup at a time. If the sauce ends up being too thin, let it sit a while and it will thicken up.

Serving suggestion:

Serve with Southwestern Cauliflower (page 157).

Variation:

If you want the mac and cheese to have a crust on top, pour the mac and cheese from the Instant Pot into an oven-safe baking dish. Top with additional cheese and bake in a 325°F oven for about 15 minutes.

Seafood

Crumb-Topped Fish Filets

Marie Skelly, Babylon, NY

Makes 4 servings

Prep. Time: 10 minutes ❧ *Baking Time: 10–12 minutes*

½ stick (¼ cup) butter, melted,
or olive oil

½ tsp. dried tarragon, or 1½ tsp. fresh
tarragon leaves

½ tsp. onion salt

1 lb. fish filets

⅔ cup dry breadcrumbs

1. In a small bowl or saucepan, mix melted butter or olive oil and tarragon.

2. Place fish in lightly greased baking pan. Spoon half of butter mixture over top.

3. Mix remaining butter mixture with breadcrumbs. Sprinkle over fish.

4. Bake at 350°F for 10–12 minutes, or until fish flakes easily with fork.

Seasoned Salmon

Charmaine Caesar, Lancaster, PA

Makes 3 servings

Prep. Time: 10 minutes ⚬ *Baking Time: 15–20 minutes*

1 lb. salmon filet

3 Tbsp. lemon juice

2 Tbsp. fresh dill, or 2 tsp. dried dill weed

2 Tbsp. minced garlic, or powdered garlic to taste

3 slices onion on top

1. Line a 9 × 13-inch baking pan with foil. Spray foil with nonstick spray.

2. Place fish on foil. Sprinkle with lemon juice.

3. Sprinkle with dill and garlic. Place onion slices on top.

4. Cover with second sheet of foil.

5. Bake at 450°F for 15–20 minutes, or until fish flakes easily. (Salmon is still pink after being fully cooked.)

Serving suggestion:

This would go well served with Broccoli with Garlic and Lemon, which can be found on page 154.

Maple-Glazed Salmon

Jenelle Miller, Marion, SD

Makes 6 servings

Prep. Time: 10 minutes   *Grilling Time: 8–9 minutes*

2 tsp. paprika
2 tsp. chili powder
½ tsp. ground cumin
½ tsp. brown sugar
6 (4-oz.) salmon fillets
I tsp. kosher salt, *optional*
I Tbsp. maple syrup

1. Spray grill rack with cooking spray. Heat grill to medium.

2. Combine first four ingredients in a small bowl.

3. Sprinkle fillets with salt if you wish. Rub with paprika mixture.

4. Place fish on grill rack. Grill 7 minutes.

5. Drizzle fish with maple syrup.

6. Grill 1–2 minutes more, or until fish flakes easily when tested with a fork.

Variation:

If you want to bake this, bake at 450°F for 15–18 minutes, or until fish flakes easily. Drizzle with the maple syrup and place under the broiler for 1–2 minutes

STOVETOP

Quick Wild Salmon Cakes

Willard E. Roth, Elkhart, IN

Makes 4 servings

Prep. Time: 10 minutes ⚬ Cooking Time: 10 minutes

15-oz. can wild-caught
Alaskan pink salmon

1 large egg

1 cup crushed wheat saltines

½ cup chopped onion

Additional seasonings, *optional*

1 Tbsp. olive oil

1. In a medium-sized mixing bowl, mix salmon, egg, saltines, and onion with your hands. Add any other seasonings that you wish.

2. Form into four balls and flatten into cakes.

3. Heat oil in skillet, preferably cast-iron. Brown cakes on medium-high heat for five minutes. Turn over and brown an additional five minutes on medium-high.

STOVETOP

Shrimp with Sun-Dried Tomatoes

Josie Healy, Middle Village, NY

Makes 3–4 servings

Prep. Time: 10 minutes ⚶ *Cooking Time: 7–10 minutes*

2 Tbsp. olive oil

1 lb. cleaned and peeled shrimp

2 cloves garlic, minced

¼ cup white wine

6–8 sun-dried tomatoes, chopped
(use dry tomatoes, not in oil)

1. Place olive oil in large skillet and heat. Carefully add shrimp and garlic, being careful not to splatter yourself with the hot oil.

2. Sauté, stirring constantly, until shrimp is slightly pink and garlic is softened.

3. Stir in wine and sun-dried tomatoes. Cook another 1–2 minutes over low heat.

4. If you'd like more liquid, add ¼ cup water, more wine, or chicken stock.

Serving suggestion:

Serve over rice or pasta.

Tuna Noodle Casserole

Hope Comerford, Clinton Township, MI

Makes 8 servings

Prep. Time: 10 minutes ⚬ *Cooking Time: 2 minutes*

4 cups chicken broth

1 tsp. sea salt

1 tsp. garlic powder

1 tsp. onion powder

¼ tsp. pepper

12 oz. egg noodles

2 (5-oz.) cans tuna, drained

2 cups frozen peas and carrots, thawed

½ cup heavy cream

3 cups shredded white cheddar cheese

1. Pour the broth, salt, garlic powder, onion powder, and pepper into the inner pot of the Instant Pot. Stir.

2. Pour in the egg noodles and push under the liquid. Sprinkle the tuna on top.

3. Secure the lid and set the vent to sealing.

4. Manually set the cook time for 2 minutes on high pressure.

5. When cook time is up, let the pressure release naturally.

6. When the pin drops, remove the lid and stir in the peas and carrots.

7. SLOWLY stir in the heavy cream, a little at a time, so it does not curdle.

8. Stir in the shredded cheese, a little at a time. Press Cancel.

9. Let the mixture thicken with the lid off until desired thickness is reached. It will thicken as it cools.

Soups, Stews & Chilies

Chicken Spinach Soup

Carna Reitz, Remington, VA

Makes 4–6 servings

Prep. Time: 5 minutes   Cooking Time: 20 minutes

6½ cups chicken broth, *divided*

2 cups cooked chicken

1–2 cups frozen chopped spinach

Salt and pepper to taste

½ cup flour

1. Put 6 cups broth, chicken, spinach, and salt and pepper in a large stock pot. Bring to a boil.

2. Meanwhile, mix flour and remaining ½ cup broth together in a jar. Put on lid and shake until smooth. When soup is boiling, slowly pour flour mixture into soup to thicken, stirring constantly.

3. Continue stirring and cooking until soup thickens.

Slow-Cooker Chicken Noodle Soup

Jennifer J. Gehman, Harrisburg, PA

Makes 6–8 servings

Prep. Time: 5–10 minutes ⚬ *Cooking Time: 3–8 hours* ⚬ *Ideal slow-cooker size: 5-qt.*

2 cups cubed uncooked chicken, dark or white meat

15¼-oz. can corn, or 2 cups frozen corn

1 cup green beans

10 cups low-sodium chicken broth

½ pkg. dry kluski (or other very sturdy) noodles

1. Combine all ingredients except noodles in slow cooker.

2. Cover. Cook on High 3–4 hours or on Low 6–8 hours.

3. Two hours before end of cooking time, stir in noodles.

Easy Chicken Tortilla Soup

Becky Harder, Monument, CO

Makes 6–8 servings

Prep. Time: 5–10 minutes ⚬ *Cooking Time: 8 hours* ⚬ *Ideal slow-cooker size: 4- to 5-qt.*

4 chicken breast halves

2 (15-oz.) cans black beans, undrained

2 (15-oz.) cans Mexican-style stewed tomatoes, or Ro-Tel Diced Tomatoes and Green Chilies

1 cup salsa (mild, medium, or hot, whichever you prefer)

4-oz. can chopped green chilies

14½-oz. can tomato sauce

Tortilla chips

Shredded cheese, optional

1. Combine all ingredients except chips in large slow cooker.

2. Cover. Cook on Low 8 hours.

3. Just before serving, remove chicken breasts and slice into bite-sized pieces. Stir into soup.

4. Put a handful of tortilla chips in each individual soup bowl. Ladle soup over chips. Top with optional shredded cheese, if desired.

White Chicken Chili

Hope Comerford, Clinton Township, MI

Makes 4–6 servings

Prep. Time: 5 minutes ⚬ *Cooking Time: 14 minutes*

2 (15-ounce) cans great northern beans, undrained

I large sweet onion, chopped

16-oz. jar of your favorite salsa

I Tbsp. cumin

I tsp. sea salt

¼ tsp. pepper

2 cups chicken stock

2 lb. boneless, skinless chicken breasts

8 oz. shredded pepper Jack cheese

8 oz. shredded Monterey Jack cheese

1. Place the beans, chopped onion, salsa, cumin, salt, pepper, and chicken stock into the inner pot of the Instant Pot, then place the chicken on top.

2. Secure the lid and set the vent to sealing. Manually set the cook time for 14 minutes on high pressure.

3. When cook time is up, manually release the pressure. When the pin drops, remove the lid.

4. Remove the chicken breasts and shred the meat between two forks. Stir it back through the contents of the inner pot, along with the shredded pepper Jack and Monterey Jack cheeses.

Serving suggestion:
This is very good with slices of avocado and crushed tortilla chips on top.

STOVETOP

Potato-Cheese Soup

Mary Kathryn Yoder, Harrisonville, MO

Makes 5 servings

Prep. Time: 20 minutes ⚘ *Cooking Time: 20 minutes*

4 medium-sized potatoes, peeled
and cut into chunks

4 slices bacon

I small onion, *optional*

4 cups milk

¾ tsp. salt

Pepper to taste

¾ cup shredded cheese, your
choice of flavors

1. Place potato chunks in a saucepan. Add 1 inch water. Cover and cook over low heat until very tender.

2. Meanwhile, cut bacon into 1-inch lengths. Place in a large saucepan, along with the onion if you wish. Cook until tender.

3. When potatoes become tender, mash in their cooking water.

4. Add mashed potatoes and milk to bacon, and onion if using.

5. Stir in salt, pepper, and cheese. Cook over low heat, stirring occasionally to distribute cheese as it melts.

6. Soup is ready when cheese is melted and soup is hot.

Tips:

1. When you mash the potatoes, you can let them be a little lumpy. That adds interesting texture to the soup.

2. You can use leftover mashed potatoes to make this recipe if you have them.

Broccoli Rabe & Sausage Soup

Carlene Horne, Bedford, NH

Makes 4 servings

Prep. Time: 15 minutes ⚬ *Cooking Time: 15 minutes*

2 Tbsp. olive oil

1 onion, chopped

1 lb. sweet or spicy sausage, casing removed, sliced

1 bunch broccoli rabe, approximately 5 cups chopped

32 oz. carton chicken broth

1 cup water

8-oz. frozen tortellini

1. Heat olive oil in a soup pot.

2. Add onions and sausage and sauté until tender.

3. Add broccoli rabe and sauté a few more minutes.

4. Pour broth and water into pan; bring to simmer.

5. Add tortellini and cook a few minutes until tender.

Tips:

1. Substitute any green such as Swiss chard, kale, or spinach for the broccoli rabe.
2. Serve with grated cheese and crusty bread.

Sausage Chili

STOVETOP

Norma I. Gehman, Ephrata, PA

Makes 4–6 servings

Prep. Time: 15 minutes ⚬ *Cooking Time: 15 minutes*

1 lb. loose sausage
¼ cup diced onion
2 Tbsp. flour
15½-oz. can chili-style beans with liquid
14½-oz. can diced tomatoes, undrained

1. Brown sausage in a large stockpot.

2. Add diced onion. Cook over medium heat until tender.

3. When onion is cooked, sprinkle flour over mixture. Stir until flour is absorbed.

4. Add chili beans and diced tomatoes with juice. Mix well.

5. Simmer, covered, for 15 minutes.

Note:

This recipe tastes even better when warmed up a day later.

Variation:

For more zip, use hot Italian sausage.

Serving suggestions:

1. Crumble corn chips into the bottom of each serving bowl. Spoon chili over top of chips. Or crumble corn chips over top of each individual serving.

2. Grate your favorite cheese over top of each individual serving.

STOVETOP

Meatball Tortellini Soup

Lucille Amos, Greensboro, NC

Makes 4 servings

Prep. Time: 5 minutes ⚹ *Cooking Time: 20–25 minutes*

14-oz. can beef broth
12 frozen Italian meatballs
1 cup stewed tomatoes
11-oz. can Mexican-style corn, drained
1 cup frozen cheese tortellini
(about 20)

1. Bring broth to boil in a large stockpot.

2. Add meatballs. Cover and reduce heat. Simmer 5 minutes.

3. Add tomatoes and corn. Cover and simmer 5 minutes more.

4. Add tortellini. Cover and simmer 5 more minutes, or until tortellini is tender.

Quick and Easy Chili

Carolyn Spohn, Shawnee, KS

Makes 3–4 servings

Prep. Time: 10 minutes   *Cooking Time: 25 minutes*

½ lb. ground beef, or turkey, browned and drained

1 medium-sized onion, chopped

2 cloves garlic, minced

2 (15-oz.) cans chili-style beans with liquid

8-oz. can tomato sauce

1. Brown ground beef in a large skillet.

2. Drain, leaving about 1 tsp. drippings in pan. Sauté onions and garlic until softened.

3. Add beans, with liquid, and the tomato sauce. Bring to a slow boil.

4. Reduce heat to simmer and cook for 15 minutes.

5. Return meat to skillet. Heat together for 5 minutes.

Tip:

Leftovers makes good chili dogs.

Nancy's Vegetable Beef Soup

Nancy Graves, Manhattan, KS

Makes 8 servings

Prep. Time: 5 minutes ⚶ *Cooking Time: 4–8 hours* ⚶ *Ideal slow-cooker size: 8-qt.*

2-lb. roast, cubed, or 2 lb. stewing meat

15-oz. can corn

15-oz. can green beans

1-lb. bag frozen peas

40-oz. can stewed tomatoes

5 tsp. beef bouillon powder

Tabasco to taste

½ tsp. salt

10–12 cups water

1. Combine all ingredients in the slow cooker crock. Do not drain vegetables.

2. Add water.

3. Cover and cook on Low for 8 hours or High for 4 hours, or until meat is tender and vegetables are soft.

Mexican Beef and Barley Soup

Rebecca B. Stoltzfus, Lititz, PA

Makes 4–6 servings

Prep. Time: 10 minutes ⚬ Cooking Time: 35 minutes

STOVETOP

1 lb. lean ground beef
1 small onion, chopped
1 Tbsp. olive oil
3 cups low-sodium beef broth
2 cups chunky salsa
½ cup quick cooking barley
2 (15-oz.) cans red kidney beans, rinsed and drained
4 Tbsp. sour cream
Paprika

1. In 12-inch skillet, brown beef and onion in oil, breaking up with a fork until no longer pink. Drain.

2. Add broth, salsa, and barley. Bring to a boil.

3. Reduce heat to medium and cook uncovered for 15 minutes.

4. Add beans and heat through.

5. Ladle into bowls. Garnish with dollops of sour cream dusted with paprika.

Variations:

1. If you want to use pearl barley, add an extra 1½ cups broth or water, and cook an additional 40 minutes.

2. To increase Mexican flavor to your taste, add some cumin, chili powder, or cayenne.

Creamy Broccoli Soup

SuAnne Burkholder, Millersburg, OH

Makes 3–4 servings

Prep. Time: 10–15 minutes   *Cooking Time: 15–20 minutes*

4 cups milk, *divided*

1 Tbsp. chicken-flavored soup base

1½ cups cut-up broccoli

2 Tbsp. cornstarch

Salt to taste

1. Heat 3 cups milk and chicken base in a stockpot over low heat until hot.

2. Meanwhile, place cut-up broccoli in a microwave-safe dish. Add 1 tablespoon water. Cover. Microwave on High for 1½ minutes. Stir. Repeat until broccoli becomes bright green and just-tender. Be careful not to overcook it! Drain broccoli of liquid.

3. In a small bowl, or in a jar with a tight-fitting lid, mix 1 cup milk and cornstarch until smooth. Slowly add to hot milk mixture.

4. Simmer gently, stirring constantly. When slightly thickened, add broccoli and salt.

Variation:

To keep this vegetarian, sub a vegetable base for a the chicken-flavored soup base.

Tomato Basil Soup

STOVETOP

Barbara Kuhns, Millersburg, OH

Makes 4–6 servings

Prep. Time: 15 minutes ❧ *Cooking Time: 25 minutes*

1 stick (8 Tbsp.) butter
¼ cup finely chopped onion
2 (10½-oz.) cans condensed tomato soup
2 cups tomato sauce
6-oz. can tomato paste
2 (14½-oz.) cans chicken broth
3 tsp. basil
¼ cup brown sugar
Cloves of garlic, minced, *optional*
1 cup heavy whipping cream
⅓ cup flour

1. Melt butter in soup pot.

2. Add and sauté onion until softened.

3. Add condensed soup, sauce, paste, broth, basil, brown sugar, and garlic (if using).

4. Cook, covered, until hot.

5. Whisk together cream and flour.

6. Add to soup and heat gently, stirring, until soup is steaming and thick. Do not boil.

Serving suggestion:
Serve with cheesy garlic bread.

Flavorful Tomato Soup

Shari Ladd, Hudson, MI

Makes 4 servings

Prep. Time: 10 minutes ⚬ *Cooking Time: 20 minutes*

2 Tbsp. chopped onions

1 Tbsp. extra-virgin olive oil

3 Tbsp. flour

2 tsp. sugar

½ tsp. pepper

¼ tsp. dried basil

½ tsp. dried oregano

¼ tsp. dried thyme

1 qt. stewed tomatoes, no salt added, undrained

2 cups skim milk

1. Sauté onions in oil in stockpot.

2. Stir in flour and seasonings.

3. Stir in stewed tomatoes, stirring constantly. Bring to a boil and boil 1 minute.

4. Add milk. If soup is too thick, add a little water. Stir well.

5. Simmer 10 minutes but do not boil.

Veggie Minestrone

Dorothy VanDeest, Memphis, TN

Makes 8 servings

Prep. Time: 5 minutes ⚬ *Cooking Time: 4 minutes*

2 Tbsp. olive oil

1 large onion, chopped

1 clove garlic, minced

4 cups low-sodium chicken or vegetable stock

16-oz. can kidney beans, rinsed and drained

14½-oz. can no-salt-added diced tomatoes

2 medium carrots, sliced thin

¼ tsp. dried oregano

¼ tsp. pepper

½ cup whole wheat elbow macaroni, uncooked

4 oz. fresh spinach

½ cup grated Parmesan cheese

1. Set the Instant Pot to the Sauté function and heat the olive oil.

2. When the olive oil is heated, add the onion and garlic to the inner pot and sauté for 5 minutes.

3. Press Cancel and add the stock, kidney beans, tomatoes, carrots, oregano, and pepper. Gently pour in the macaroni, but do not stir. Just push the noodles gently under the liquid.

4. Secure the lid and set the vent to sealing.

5. Manually set the cook time for 4 minutes on high pressure.

6. When the cooking time is over, manually release the pressure and remove the lid when the pin drops.

7. Stir in the spinach and let wilt a few minutes.

8. Sprinkle 1 tablespoon grated Parmesan on each individual bowl of this soup. Enjoy!

Mediterranean Lentil Soup

Marcia S. Myer, Manheim, PA

Makes 6 servings

Prep. Time: 10 minutes ⚬ *Cooking Time: 18 minutes*

2 Tbsp. olive oil

2 large onions, chopped

1 carrot, chopped

1 cup uncooked lentils

½ tsp. dried thyme

½ tsp. dried marjoram

3 cups low-sodium chicken stock or vegetable stock

14½-oz. can diced no-salt-added tomatoes

¼ cup chopped fresh parsley

¼ cup sherry, *optional*

⅔ cup grated low-fat cheese, *optional*

1. Set the Instant Pot to the Sauté function, then heat up the olive oil.

2. Sauté the onions and carrot until the onions are translucent, about 5 minutes.

3. Press the Cancel button, then add the lentils, thyme, marjoram, chicken stock, and canned tomatoes.

4. Secure the lid and set the vent to sealing.

5. Manually set the cook time to 18 minutes at high pressure.

6. When the cooking time is over, manually release the pressure.

7. When the pin drops, stir in the parsley and sherry (if using).

8. When serving, add a sprinkle of grated low-fat cheese if you wish.

INSTANT POT

Cannellini Bean Soup

Hope Comerford, Clinton Township, MI

Makes 6–8 servings

Prep. Time: 10 minutes ⚹ Cooking Time: 6 minutes

2 Tbsp. extra-virgin olive oil

4 cloves garlic, sliced very thin

1 small onion, chopped

2 heads escarole, well washed and cut medium-fine (about 8 cups)

4 (15½-oz.) cans cannellini beans, rinsed and drained

8 cups low-sodium chicken stock

3 basil leaves, chopped fine

Parmesan cheese shavings, *optional*

1. Set the Instant Pot to Sauté and heat the olive oil.

2. Sauté the garlic, onion, and escarole until the onion is translucent.

3. Hit the Cancel button on your Instant Pot and add the beans and chicken stock.

4. Secure the lid and set the vent to sealing.

5. Manually set the time for 6 minutes on high pressure.

6. When the cooking time is over, let the pressure release naturally. Remove the lid when the pin drops and spoon into serving bowls.

7. Top each bowl with a sprinkle of the chopped basil leaves and a few Parmesan shavings (if using).

Three-Bean Chili

Chris Kaczynski, Schenectady, NY

Makes 6 servings

Prep. Time: 10 minutes ⚬ *Cooking Time: 5 minutes*

1 medium onion, diced

16-oz. can red kidney beans, drained

16-oz. can black beans, drained

16-oz. can white kidney or garbanzo beans, drained

14-oz. can crushed tomatoes

14-oz. can diced tomatoes

1 cup medium salsa

1¼-oz. pkg. dry chili seasoning

1 Tbsp. sugar

1. Place all ingredients into the inner pot of the Instant Pot.

2. Secure the lid and set the vent to sealing. Manually set the cook time for 5 minutes on high pressure.

3. When cook time is up, let the pressure release naturally for 10 minutes, then manually release the remaining pressure.

Vegetables & Side Dishes

Roasted Baby Carrots

OVEN

Melanie Mohler, Ephrata, PA

Makes 4–5 servings

Prep. Time: 5–10 minutes *Cooking Time: 10–15 minutes*

1 lb. baby carrots
1 Tbsp. olive oil
1 Tbsp. dried dill weed
Salt

1. Preheat oven to 475°F.

2. If using thick baby carrots, slice in half lengthwise. Otherwise leave as is.

3. In a large bowl, combine olive oil and dill. Add carrots and toss to coat.

4. In a 10 × 15-inch baking pan, spread carrots in a single layer.

5. Roast, uncovered, about 10 minutes or until carrots are just tender, stirring once.

6. Sprinkle with salt before serving.

Corn Extraordinary

Judy Newman, Saint Mary's, ON

Makes 6 servings

Prep. Time: 5–7 minutes ⚹ *Cooking Time: 4–6 minutes*

2 cloves garlic

¼ cup chives

2 tsp. olive oil

4 cups fresh corn (best if cut straight off the cob), or 3 (15¼-oz.) cans no-salt-added corn

Pinch pepper

1. Chop garlic and chives.

2. Heat oil in large skillet over medium heat. Gently sauté garlic. (Reserve chives.)

3. Add corn. Sauté 3–5 minutes.

4. Season to taste with pepper and chives.

Corn with Bacon

Mary Jane Musser, Narvon, PA

Makes 6 servings

Prep. Time: 10 minutes ⚹ *Baking Time: 35 minutes*

4 cups fresh, or frozen, corn
1 tsp. salt
¼ tsp. pepper
1½ tsp. sugar
1 cup finely diced uncooked bacon

1. Place corn in a 1½-quart greased baking dish.

2. Stir in salt, pepper, and sugar.

3. Spread bacon over top of corn.

4. Bake uncovered at 350°F for 35 minutes, or until bacon is crisp.

INSTANT POT

Creamed Corn

Hope Comerford, Clinton Township, MI

Makes 6 servings

Prep. Time: 5 minutes   Cooking Time: 3 minutes

8 oz. cream cheese, cubed

½ cup heavy cream

1 stick butter, chopped into 8 tablespoons

24 oz. frozen corn

1 Tbsp. sugar

¼ tsp. dried mustard

¼ tsp. salt

⅛ tsp. pepper

1. Place all ingredients into the inner pot of the Instant Pot as listed.

2. Secure the lid and set the vent to sealing.

3. Manually set the cook time for 3 minutes.

4. When cook time is up, manually release the pressure.

5. Remove the lid, stir, and enjoy!

Variations:

You can use different flavored cream cheeses to change the flavor of your creamed corn.

You can add in diced green chilies or jalapeños to give your creamed corn a kick!

You can add crumbled cooked bacon for some extra goodness!

Broccoli with Garlic and Lemon

Jan Moore, Wellsville, KS
Leona Yoder, Hartville, OH

Makes 4–5 servings

Prep. Time: 10 minutes ⚬ *Cooking Time: 10–15 minutes*

4½ cups fresh broccoli florets

¼–½ cup water

1 Tbsp. extra-virgin olive oil

1 clove garlic, crushed,
or 1½ tsp. jarred minced garlic

Juice and grated peel from ½ lemon

Grated Parmesan cheese, *optional*

1. Place broccoli and water in a good-sized saucepan. Cover and cook over medium-high heat, stirring occasionally for several minutes until broccoli is crisp-tender. Add more water if necessary to prevent scorching, but only a small amount.

2. Drain excess liquid from skillet. Push broccoli to one side and add olive oil and garlic to the other side. Cook for about 10–20 seconds, or until garlic begins to turn color and smell fragrant.

3. Toss all together.

4. Stir in lemon juice and peel.

5. When ready to serve, top with Parmesan cheese if you wish.

Cheesy Cauliflower

Joan Erwin, Sparks, NV

Makes 4–5 servings

Prep. Time: 5–10 minutes *Cooking Time: 10 minutes*

I head cauliflower

I Tbsp. water

I cup mayonnaise

I Tbsp. prepared mustard

½ cup chopped green or red onions

I cup shredded Monterey Jack and cheddar cheeses, combined, or one of the two

1. Place whole cauliflower head in microwavable glass baking dish. Add water. Cover. Microwave on High for 9 minutes, until crisp-cooked.

2. Meanwhile, combine mayonnaise, mustard, and onions in a small bowl. Spread over cooked cauliflower. Sprinkle with cheese.

3. Cover and microwave on High for 1 minute, or until cheese is melted.

Variation:

You may break the cauliflower into florets and proceed with Step 1.

Southwestern Cauliflower

INSTANT POT

Hope Comerford, Clinton Township, MI

Makes 6–8 servings

Prep. Time: 5 minutes ⚭ *Cooking Time: 1 minute*

1 cup water

1 large head cauliflower, cut into florets

1 Tbsp. olive oil

½ tsp. smoked paprika

½ tsp. chili powder

½ tsp. cumin

½ tsp. sea salt

¼ tsp. oregano

⅛ tsp. black pepper

1. Pour the water into the inner pot of the Instant Pot, then place the steamer basket on top.

2. Put the cauliflower florets into a medium-sized bowl and pour over the olive oil and sprinkle the seasonings over the top. Toss to coat everything well. Pour into the steamer basket.

3. Secure the lid and set the vent to sealing. Manually set the cook time for 1 minute on high pressure.

4. When cook time is up, manually release the pressure.

5. When the pin drops, carefully remove the lid and serve the cauliflower.

Absolutely Creamy Spinach

Vicki J. Hill, Memphis, TN

Makes 9 servings

Prep. Time: 5 minutes ⚬ *Cooking Time: 8–30 minutes*

4 (10-oz.) pkgs. frozen chopped spinach, thawed and squeezed dry

8-oz. pkg. cream cheese

8 Tbsp. (1 stick) butter

Fine breadcrumbs

Sprinkle of paprika, *optional*

1. Place spinach in lightly greased 2-quart baking dish.

2. Soften cream cheese and butter in microwave for 1 minute. Beat until combined. Pour over spinach.

3. Sprinkle with crumbs, and paprika if desired.

4. Heat uncovered in oven at 350°F for 20–30 minutes, or in the microwave, covered, for 8–10 minutes.

Oven Brussels Sprouts

OVEN

Gail Martin, Elkhart, IN

Makes 8 servings

Prep. Time: 15 minutes ⚘ *Baking Time: 15–20 minutes*

1½ lb. Brussels sprouts, halved

¼ cup + 2 Tbsp. olive oil, *divided*

Juice of 1 lemon

½ tsp. salt

½ tsp. pepper

½ tsp. crushed red pepper flakes

1. In a large bowl, toss halved sprouts with 2 tablespoons olive oil.

2. Place them on a single layer on a rimmed cookie sheet.

3. Roast sprouts in the oven at 450°F, stirring twice, until crisp and lightly browned, about 15–20 minutes.

4. Whisk together in a large bowl ¼ cup oil, lemon juice, salt, pepper, and crushed red pepper.

5. Toss sprouts with dressing and serve.

Stir-Fried Asparagus

Sylvia Beiler, Lowville, NY

Makes 6 servings

Prep. Time: 5 minutes ⚘ *Cooking Time: 2–3 minutes*

1 Tbsp. canola oil

3 cups diagonally sliced asparagus

4 scallions, or green onions, sliced diagonally

1 clove garlic, minced, *optional*

1 tsp. lemon juice

1. Heat oil in pan. Add sliced vegetables and garlic, if using.

2. Stir-fry until crisp-tender.

3. Sprinkle with lemon juice. Serve immediately.

OVEN

Roasted Asparagus

Barbara Walker, Sturgis, SD

Makes 6 servings

Prep. Time: 5 minutes   *Cooking Time: 12 minutes*

1 lb. fresh asparagus spears
2–3 Tbsp. olive oil
⅛ tsp. pepper
2 Tbsp. balsamic vinegar

1. Place asparagus in bowl with olive oil. Toss together to coat asparagus.

2. Place asparagus spears on a baking sheet in a single layer. Sprinkle with pepper.

3. Roast uncovered at 450°F. Shake pan once or twice to turn spears after about 6 minutes.

4. Roast another 6 minutes, or until asparagus is tender-crisp.

5. Put on a plate and drizzle with balsamic vinegar. Serve immediately

Green Bean and Mushroom Sauté

Louise Bodziony, Sunrise Beach, MO
Clara Yoder Byler, Hartville, OH

Makes 4 servings

Prep. Time: 10 minutes ⚶ *Cooking Time: 20 minutes*

1 lb. fresh, or frozen, green beans

¾–1 cup sliced fresh mushrooms

2 Tbsp. butter

2–3 tsp. onion, or garlic, powder

4 strips bacon, cooked and crumbled, *optional*

1. Cook green beans in water to cover, just until tender.

2. Meanwhile, in a skillet sauté mushrooms in butter until tender.

3. Stir in onion, or garlic, powder.

4. Drain beans. Add to skillet and toss with mushrooms and seasonings.

5. Place in serving dish. Top with crumbled bacon if you wish.

Zesty Green Beans

June Grafl, Denver, PA

Makes 4–5 servings

Prep. Time: 2–3 minutes ✤ Cooking Time: 15–20 minutes

1 lb. fresh, or frozen, green beans
6 slices bacon, cut in pieces
½ Tbsp. prepared mustard
6 Tbsp. sugar
2 Tbsp. apple cider, or red wine, vinegar

1. Place beans in large stockpot with about an inch of water. Cover and steam until just-tender.

2. While beans are cooking, sauté bacon in a skillet. When crispy, remove from pan and drain. Reserve drippings. Crumble bacon and set aside.

3. To bacon drippings, add remaining ingredients. Bring to a boil, stirring frequently to mix well.

4. Stir bacon back into sauce.

5. Drain cooked beans. Stir sauce into drained beans.

Sweet Potato Puree

Colleen Heatwole, Burton, MI

Makes 4–6 servings

Prep. Time: 10 minutes   Cooking Time: 6 minutes

3 lb. sweet potatoes, peeled and cut into roughly 2-inch cubes

1 cup water

2 Tbsp. butter

1 tsp. salt

2 tsp. packed brown sugar

2 tsp. lemon juice

½ tsp. cinnamon

⅛ tsp. nutmeg, *optional*

1. Place the sweet potatoes and water in the inner pot of the Instant Pot.

2. Secure the lid, make sure the vent is on sealing, then manually set the cook time for 6 minutes on high pressure.

3. Manually release the pressure when the cook time is over.

4. Drain the sweet potatoes and place them in a large mixing bowl. Mash with a potato masher or hand mixer.

5. Once thoroughly mashed, add remaining ingredients.

6. Taste and adjust seasonings to taste.

7. Serve immediately while still hot.

Hometown Spanish Rice

Beverly Flatt-Getz, Warriors Mark, PA

Makes 6–8 servings

Prep. Time: 8 minutes   Cooking Time: 3 minutes

1 Tbsp. olive oil

1 large onion, chopped

1 bell pepper, chopped

2 cups long-grain rice, rinsed

1½ cups low-sodium chicken stock

28-oz. can low-sodium stewed tomatoes

Grated Parmesan cheese, *optional*

1. Set the Instant Pot to Sauté and heat the oil in the inner pot.

2. Sauté the onion and bell pepper in the inner pot for about 3–5 minutes.

3. Add the rice and continue to sauté for about 1 more minute. Press Cancel.

4. Add the chicken stock and tomatoes with their juices into the inner pot, in that order.

5. Secure the lid and set the vent to sealing.

6. Manually set the cook time for 3 minutes on high pressure.

7. When the cooking time is over, let the pressure release naturally for 10 minutes, then manually release the remaining pressure.

8. When the pin drops, remove the lid. Fluff the rice with a fork.

9. Sprinkle with Parmesan cheese, if using, just before serving.

Savory Rice

Barb Harvey, Quarryville, PA
Carna Reitz, Remington, VA

Makes 6 servings

Prep. Time: 5 minutes *Cooking Time: 30 minutes*

½–¾ stick (4–6 Tbsp.) butter
1 cup uncooked long-grain rice
2½ cups water
3 beef bouillon cubes
1 Tbsp. fresh parsley
1 Tbsp. fresh basil

1. Melt butter in good-sized saucepan over medium heat.

2. Add rice, water, and bouillon cubes. Cover and bring to a boil.

3. Turn heat to low and cook 20–25 minutes until rice is soft, stirring once.

4. Just before serving, stir in fresh herbs.

Variations:

1. Substitute 2½ cups chicken broth for the water and beef bouillon cubes.

2. Drop the fresh basil. Replace with 1 tsp. dried onion and 1 tsp. seasoned salt.

STOVETOP

Rice-Vermicelli Pilaf

Jan Mast, Lancaster, PA

Makes 4 servings

Prep. Time: 5 minutes ⚬ *Cooking Time: 30 minutes*

4 Tbsp. (½ stick) butter

I cup uncooked long-grain rice

½ cup uncooked vermicelli, broken into short pieces

2¾ cups chicken broth

2 Tbsp. parsley

1. Melt butter in a saucepan. Add rice and noodles, stirring until browned, about 3 minutes.

2. Stir in broth and bring to a boil.

3. Reduce heat, cover, and simmer 20–25 minutes, or until rice is tender.

4. Stir in parsley before serving.

Desserts

Candy Bar Cookies

Arianne Hochstetler, Goshen, IN

Makes 36 bars

Prep. Time: 15–20 minutes   Baking Time: 15 minutes

I cup brown sugar
8 Tbsp. (1 stick) butter, softened
½ cup light corn syrup
3 tsp. vanilla extract
I tsp. salt
4 cups rolled oats
½ cup peanut butter
I cup semisweet chocolate chips

1. Cream brown sugar and butter in a large bowl until fluffy.

2. Add corn syrup, vanilla, salt, and rolled oats. Mix well.

3. Spread mixture evenly in greased 9 × 13-inch pan.

4. Bake at 350°F for 15 minutes. Do not overbake.

5. Meanwhile, combine peanut butter and chocolate chips in a small bowl.

6. When the bars are done baking, immediately spread peanut butter/chocolate mixture over the hot bars so heat melts chocolate chips.

7. When cool, cut into bars and remove from pan.

OVEN

Peanut Butter Cookies

Juanita Lyndaker, Croghan, NY
Stacy Stoltzfus, Grantham, PA
Joleen Albrecht, Gladstone, MI
Doris Bachman, Putnam, IL

Makes 1–1½ dozen cookies

Prep. Time: 15 minutes   *Baking Time: 8–10 minutes per sheet*

I cup peanut butter
I cup sugar
I egg
Additional sugar

1. Mix the first three ingredients together in a medium-sized mixing bowl.

2. Break dough off with a teaspoon and shape into balls.

3. Roll each ball in granulated sugar.

4. Place on greased baking sheet. Press down with a fork, making a crisscross pattern.

5. Bake at 350°F for 8–10 minutes, or until golden brown.

Lemon Chocolate Chip Cookies

Hope Comerford, Clinton Township, MI

Makes 24 cookies

Prep. Time: 10 minutes   Baking Time: 15 minutes

1 box lemon cake mix

2 eggs

½ cup vegetable oil or coconut oil

1 cup white chocolate chips

1. Preheat the oven to 325°F.

2. In a large mixing bowl, mix the lemon cake mix, eggs, and vegetable oil. Stir in the white chocolate chips.

3. On a greased cookie sheet or parchment paper–lined cookie sheet, place 1½-tsp.-sized balls of dough 1 inch apart.

4. Bake for 15 minutes.

5. Let cool slightly, then place on a cooling rack.

Chocolate Cake in a Mug

Peggy Howell, Hinton, WV

Makes 1–2 servings

Prep. Time: 5 minutes ⚬ *Cooking Time: 3 minutes*

4 Tbsp. cake flour
4 Tbsp. sugar
2 Tbsp. cocoa
1 egg
3 Tbsp. milk
3 Tbsp. vegetable oil
Dash vanilla extract
3 Tbsp. chocolate chips

1. Add flour, sugar, and cocoa to a large coffee mug; mix well.

2. Add egg and mix thoroughly.

3. Pour in milk, oil, vanilla, and chocolate chips. Mix well.

4. Cook on High in microwave for about 3 minutes. Test for firmness by pressing on the top with a spoon. Microwave in 30 second increments until done.

5. Allow to cool a little before eating.

Tip:

After mixing, split cake batter into 2 mugs. Bake. This will give you space on top to add a scoop of ice cream to each mug.

Easy Brownies

Donna Klaassen, Whitewater, KS

Makes 36 brownies

Prep. Time: 15 minutes   *Baking Time: 25–30 minutes*

8 Tbsp. (1 stick) butter, softened

1 cup sugar

4 eggs

1 cup flour

1 can chocolate syrup

½ cup chopped walnuts, *optional*

1. In a medium mixing bowl, use an electric mixer to cream the butter and sugar together.

2. Add the eggs one at a time and beat after each addition.

3. Stir in the flour, blending well.

4. Stir in the chocolate syrup, blending well.

5. Stir in the walnuts, if using.

6. Pour into a lightly greased 9-inch square baking pan.

7. Bake at 350°F for 25–30 minutes.

8. When cooled, cut into squares with a plastic knife. (A plastic knife won't drag crumbs while cutting.)

Dark Chocolate Lava Cake

SLOW COOKER

Hope Comerford, Clinton Township, MI

Makes 8 servings

Prep. Time: 5–10 minutes · Cook Time: 2–3 hours · Ideal slow-cooker size: 4-qt.

5 eggs

1 cup dark cocoa powder

⅔ cup maple syrup

⅔ cup dark chocolate, chopped into very fine pieces or shaved

1. In a large mixing bowl, whisk the eggs and then slowly whisk in the cocoa powder, maple syrup, and dark chocolate.

2. Spray a slow-cooker crock with nonstick cooking spray.

3. Pour the egg/chocolate mixture into the crock.

4. Cover and cook on Low for 2–3 hours with some folded paper towel under the lid to collect condensation. It is done when the middle is set and bounces back up when touched.

Blueberry Swirl Cake

OVEN

Lori Lehman, Ephrata, PA

Makes 15 servings

Prep. Time: 15 minutes   *Baking Time: 30–40 minutes*

3-oz. pkg. cream cheese, softened
18¼-oz. box white cake mix
3 eggs
3 Tbsp. water
21-oz. can blueberry pie filling

1. In a large mixing bowl, beat the cream cheese until it is soft and creamy.

2. Stir in the dry cake mix, eggs, and water. Blend well with the cream cheese.

3. Pour into a greased 9 × 13-inch baking pan.

4. Pour the blueberry pie filling over the top of the batter.

5. Swirl the blueberries and batter with a knife by zigzagging through batter.

6. Bake at 350°F for 30–40 minutes, or until a tester inserted in the center comes out clean.

Banana Split Snack Cake

Marla Folkerts, Holland, OH

Makes 20–24 servings

Prep. Time: 15 minutes   *Baking Time: 30 minutes*

5 Tbsp. butter or margarine, softened

¾ cup sugar

1 egg

1 medium ripe banana, mashed

½ tsp. vanilla extract

1¼ cups flour

1 tsp. baking powder

¼ tsp. salt

⅓ cup chopped walnuts

2 cups mini marshmallows

1 cup chocolate chips

⅓ cup quartered maraschino cherries

1. Using a mixer, cream butter and sugar.

2. Beat in egg, banana, and vanilla.

3. Stir in flour, baking powder, salt, and walnuts.

4. Spread evenly into greased 9 × 13-inch baking pan. Bake at 350°F for 20 minutes.

5. Sprinkle mini marshmallows, chocolate chips, and maraschino cherries over the hot cake. Bake 10 minutes longer or until lightly browned.

Cherry Cheese Cake Tarts

Jan Mast, Lancaster, PA

Makes 18 servings

Prep. Time: 15 minutes   *Baking Time: 15–20 minutes*

18 vanilla wafers
8-oz. cream cheese, softened
3 eggs
¾ cup sugar
21-oz. can cherry pie filling

Tip:

Do not over-beat the cream cheese mixture—it needs to be heavy enough to keep the wafers at the bottom. If too much air is beaten into it, the wafers will float to the top.

1. Fill cupcake tins with 18 paper cupcake liners.

2. Place one vanilla wafer in each paper liner. Set aside.

3. Beat cream cheese just until soft and smooth. Do not overbeat.

4. Add eggs and sugar, beating until just blended. Do not overbeat.

5. Pour cream cheese mixture evenly into 18 cupcake liners, covering vanilla wafer.

6. Bake at 325°F for 15–20 minutes. Cool completely.

7. Top each cooled tart with cherry pie filling.

8. Refrigerate until ready to serve.

Variation:

1. Substitute blueberry pie filling or eliminate pie filling and use slices of assorted fresh fruits like kiwi, orange, strawberry, etc.

Swiss Coconut Custard Pie

Elsie Schlabach, Millersburg, OH

Makes 8 servings

Prep. Time: 8 minutes ⚬ *Baking Time: 50 minutes*

4 eggs, beaten

¼ cup brown sugar

¾ cup sugar

I tsp. vanilla extract

2 drops maple extract

2 cups milk

½ cup flour

½ tsp. baking powder

6 Tbsp. butter or margarine, softened

I cup coconut

1. Beat eggs in a medium mixing bowl.

2. Add sugars, extracts, milk, flour, baking powder, and butter. Beat 2 minutes.

3. Stir in coconut.

4. Pour into a greased deep-dish 12-inch pie pan. Bake at 350°F for 50 minutes until center of pie is set.

Tip:

After it's baked, the crust will be on the bottom, custard in the middle, and coconut on top. An easy trick to get a pie!

Not Yo' Mama's Banana Pudding

Barbara Shie, Colorado Springs, CO

Makes 20 servings

Prep. Time: 20–30 minutes

2 (7¼-oz.) pkgs. Pepperidge Farm
Chessmen Cookies

6–8 bananas, peeled and sliced

2 Tbsp. lemon juice

2 cups milk

5-oz. box instant French vanilla pudding

8-oz. pkg. cream cheese, softened

14-oz. can sweetened condensed milk

12-oz. frozen whipped topping, thawed

1. Line the bottom of 9 × 13-inch pan with 1 bag of cookies.

2. Gently mix the bananas with lemon juice to prevent browning.

3. Layer bananas on top of cookies.

4. In a small bowl, combine milk and pudding mix and blend well until thick. Set aside.

5. Using a large bowl, combine cream cheese and condensed milk together and mix until smooth.

6. Fold the whipped topping into the cream cheese mixture.

7. Add the pudding to the cream cheese mixture and stir until well blended.

8. Pour the mixture over the cookies and bananas.

9. Cover with the remaining cookies.

10. Refrigerate until ready to serve.

Cookies-and-Cream Fluff

Ruth Hofstetter, Versailles, MO

Makes 6 servings

Prep. Time: 5–10 minutes

2 cups cold milk

3-oz. pkg. instant vanilla pudding mix

8 oz. frozen whipped topping, thawed

15 chocolate cream-filled sandwich cookies, broken into chunks

Additional broken cookies, *optional*

1. In a bowl, whisk the milk and pudding mix for 2 minutes, or until slightly thickened.

2. Fold in the whipped topping and cookies.

3. Spoon into dessert dishes.

4. When ready to serve, top with additional cookies if you wish.

Candy Bar Apple Salad

Jennifer Archer, Kalona, IA

Makes 10–12 servings

Prep. Time: 15–20 minutes

3-oz. pkg. instant vanilla pudding
I cup milk
8 oz. frozen whipped topping, thawed
6 apples, peeled or unpeeled, diced
6 Snickers® bars, diced or broken

1. In a large mixing bowl, mix the pudding mix with the milk.

2. Fold in the whipped topping.

3. Fold in the chopped apples and Snickers.

4. Cover and refrigerate until ready to serve.

S'mores Dip

Jessalyn Wantland, Napoleon, OH
Melissa Wenger, Orrville, OH

Makes 3 cups

Prep. Time: 20 minutes

2 (8-oz. pkgs.) cream cheese, softened
16 Tbsp. (2 sticks) butter
1 Tbsp. vanilla extract
4 Tbsp. brown sugar
1½ cups confectioners' sugar
12-oz. pkg. miniature chocolate chips
Chocolate graham crackers
or graham cracker sticks

1. Beat cream cheese and butter together until fluffy.

2. Stir in vanilla, sugars, and chocolate chips.

3. Refrigerate. Serve with chocolate graham crackers or graham cracker sticks.

Tips:

1. Before serving, form into a mound and top with 1½ cup pecans.

2. Margarine is not a good substitute for butter in this recipe!

Apple Dippers

Christine Lucke, Aumsville, OR

Makes 1 cup

Prep. Time: 15 minutes

8-oz. pkg. cream cheese
2 tsp. milk
½ cup brown sugar
5 apples, sliced

1. Whip cream cheese, milk, and brown sugar to a smooth, fluffy consistency.

2. Serve sliced apples with cream cheese and brown sugar for dipping.

Tips:

1. I like Braeburn or Cameo apples.
2. You can use some lemon juice and water to keep the apples from browning, but I just slice right before serving and the Braeburns don't turn brown before they are eaten.

Caramel Corn

Hope Comerford, Clinton Township, MI

Makes 5–6 servings

Prep. Time: 3 minutes ⚘ *Cook Time: 15 minutes*

2 Tbsp. coconut oil

½ cup popcorn kernels

½ tsp. sea salt

Caramel sauce:

8 Tbsp. (1 stick) sweet cream salted butter

½ cup light brown sugar

2 Tbsp. heavy cream

1 tsp. vanilla extract

¼ tsp. baking soda

1. Set the Instant Pot to the Sauté function. Add the coconut oil and let it melt.

2. When the oil is melted, add the popcorn kernels, stir, then secure the lid. Let it cook for about 3 minutes, or until you do not hear kernels popping.

3. Press Cancel and move the popcorn to a bowl. Toss with the salt.

4. Place the inner pot back into the Instant Pot base and press the Sauté function.

5. Add the butter and let it melt. Once it's melted, add the brown sugar and heavy cream. When the sugar is dissolved, add the vanilla and baking soda. Continue to cook until the sauce has thickened into caramel.

6. Press Cancel on the Instant Pot. Add the popcorn back into the inner pot and gently stir to coat it with the caramel sauce.

7. Line a baking sheet with parchment paper, foil, or a silicone mat. Pour the caramel corn onto the baking sheet in a single layer and let it cool.

Metric Equivalent Measurements

If you're accustomed to using metric measurements, I don't want you to be inconvenienced by the imperial measurements I use in this book.

Use this handy chart, too, to figure out the size of the slow cooker you'll need for each recipe.

Weight (Dry Ingredients)

1 oz		30 g
4 oz	¼ lb	120 g
8 oz	½ lb	240 g
12 oz	¾ lb	360 g
16 oz	1 lb	480 g
32 oz	2 lb	960 g

Slow-Cooker Sizes

1-quart	0.96 l
2-quart	1.92 l
3-quart	2.88 l
4-quart	3.84 l
5-quart	4.80 l
6-quart	5.76 l
7-quart	6.72 l
8-quart	7.68 l

Volume (Liquid Ingredients)

½ tsp.		2 ml
1 tsp.		5 ml
1 Tbsp.	½ fl oz	15 ml
2 Tbsp.	1 fl oz	30 ml
¼ cup	2 fl oz	60 ml
⅓ cup	3 fl oz	80 ml
½ cup	4 fl oz	120 ml
⅔ cup	5 fl oz	160 ml
¾ cup	6 fl oz	180 ml
1 cup	8 fl oz	240 ml
1 pt	16 fl oz	480 ml
1 qt	32 fl oz	960 ml

Length

¼ in	6 mm
½ in	13 mm
¾ in	19 mm
1 in	25 mm
6 in	15 cm
12 in	30 cm

Recipe & Ingredient Index

About the Author

Hope Comerford is a mom, wife, elementary music teacher, blogger, recipe developer, public speaker, Young Living Essential Oils essential oil enthusiast/educator, and published author. In 2013, she was diagnosed with a severe gluten intolerance and since then has spent many hours creating easy, practical, and delicious gluten-free recipes that can be enjoyed by both those who are affected by gluten and those who are not.

Growing up, Hope spent many hours in the kitchen with her Meme (grandmother) and her love for cooking grew from there. While working on her master's degree when her daughter was young, Hope turned to her slow cookers for some salvation and sanity. It was from there she began truly experimenting with recipes and quickly learned she had the ability to get a little more creative in the kitchen and develop her own recipes.

In 2010, Hope started her blog, *A Busy Mom's Slow Cooker Adventures*, to simply share the recipes she was making with her family and friends. She never imagined people all over the world would begin visiting her page and sharing her recipes with others as well. In 2013, Hope self-published her first cookbook, *Slow Cooker Recipes 10 Ingredients or Less and Gluten-Free*, and then later wrote *The Gluten-Free Slow Cooker*.

Hope became the new brand ambassador and author of Fix-It and Forget-It in mid-2016. Since then, she has brought her excitement and creativeness to the Fix-It and Forget-It brand. Through Fix-It and Forget-It, she has written *Welcome Home Super Simple Entertaining, Fix-It and Forget-It Slow Cooker Dump Dinners & Desserts, Fix-It and Forget-It Instant Pot Cookbook, Fix-It and Forget-It Freezer Meals, Welcome Home Harvest Cookbook,* and many more.

Hope lives in the city of Clinton Township, Michigan, near Metro Detroit. She has been happily married to her husband and best friend, Justin, since 2008. Together they have two children, Ella and Gavin, who are her motivation, inspiration, and heart. In her spare time, Hope enjoys traveling, singing, cooking, reading books, spending time with friends and family, and relaxing.